GRAPHIC SCIENCE AND ENGINEERING IN ACTION

THE AMAZING WORK OF SCIENTISTS

WITH MAX AXIOM
SUPER SCIENTIST

by Agnieszka Biskup

illustrated by Marcelo Baez

Consultant:
Jim Austin
Editor, *Science* Careers
American Association for the Advancement of Science

CAPSTONE PRESS
a capstone imprint

Graphic Library is published by Capstone Press,
1710 Roe Crest Drive, North Mankato, Minnesota 56003
www.capstonepub.com

Library of Congress Cataloging-in-Publication Data
Biskup, Agnieszka.
    The amazing work of scientists with Max Axiom, super scientist / by Agnieszka Biskup.
       pages cm. — (Graphic science and engineering in action.)
    Summary: "In graphic novel format, follows the adventures of Max Axiom as he reveals
what scientists do and how they work"— Provided by publisher.
    Includes bibliographical references and index.
    ISBN 978-1-4296-9936-5 (library binding)
    ISBN 978-1-62065-701-0 (paperback)
    ISBN 978-1-4765-1588-5 (ebook PDF)
1. Science—Methodology—Comic books, strips, etc.—Juvenile literature.
2. Scientists—Comic books, strips, etc.—Juvenile literature. 3. Graphic novels. I. Title.

   Q180.55.M4B57 2013
   502.3—dc23   2012028442

Editor
Mari Bolte

Designer
Ted Williams

Media Researcher
Wanda Winch

Production Specialist
Laura Manthe

Photo credit: NASA, 7

Printed in the United States of America in Stevens Point, Wisconsin.
022014   008058R

TABLE OF CONTENTS

SECTION 1

ADVENTURES IN SCIENCE --------- 4

SECTION 2

STUDYING SCIENTISTS ------------- 8

SECTION 3

A GATHERING
OF GREAT MINDS ----------------- 26

More about Scientists 28
Glossary 30
Read More 31
Internet Sites 31
Index 32

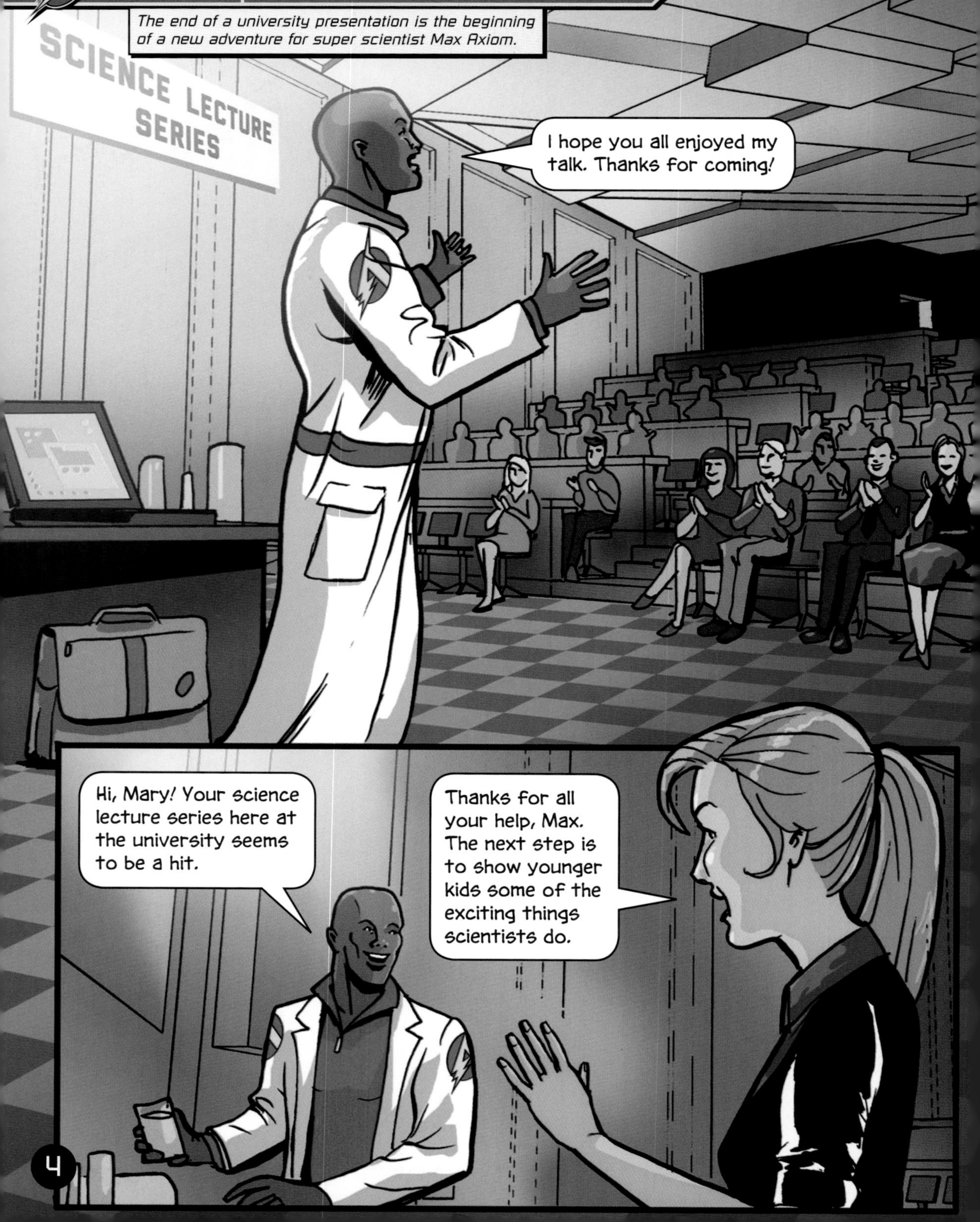
The end of a university presentation is the beginning of a new adventure for super scientist Max Axiom.
SCIENCE LECTURE SERIES
I hope you all enjoyed my talk. Thanks for coming!
Hi, Mary! Your science lecture series here at the university seems to be a hit.
Thanks for all your help, Max. The next step is to show younger kids some of the exciting things scientists do.

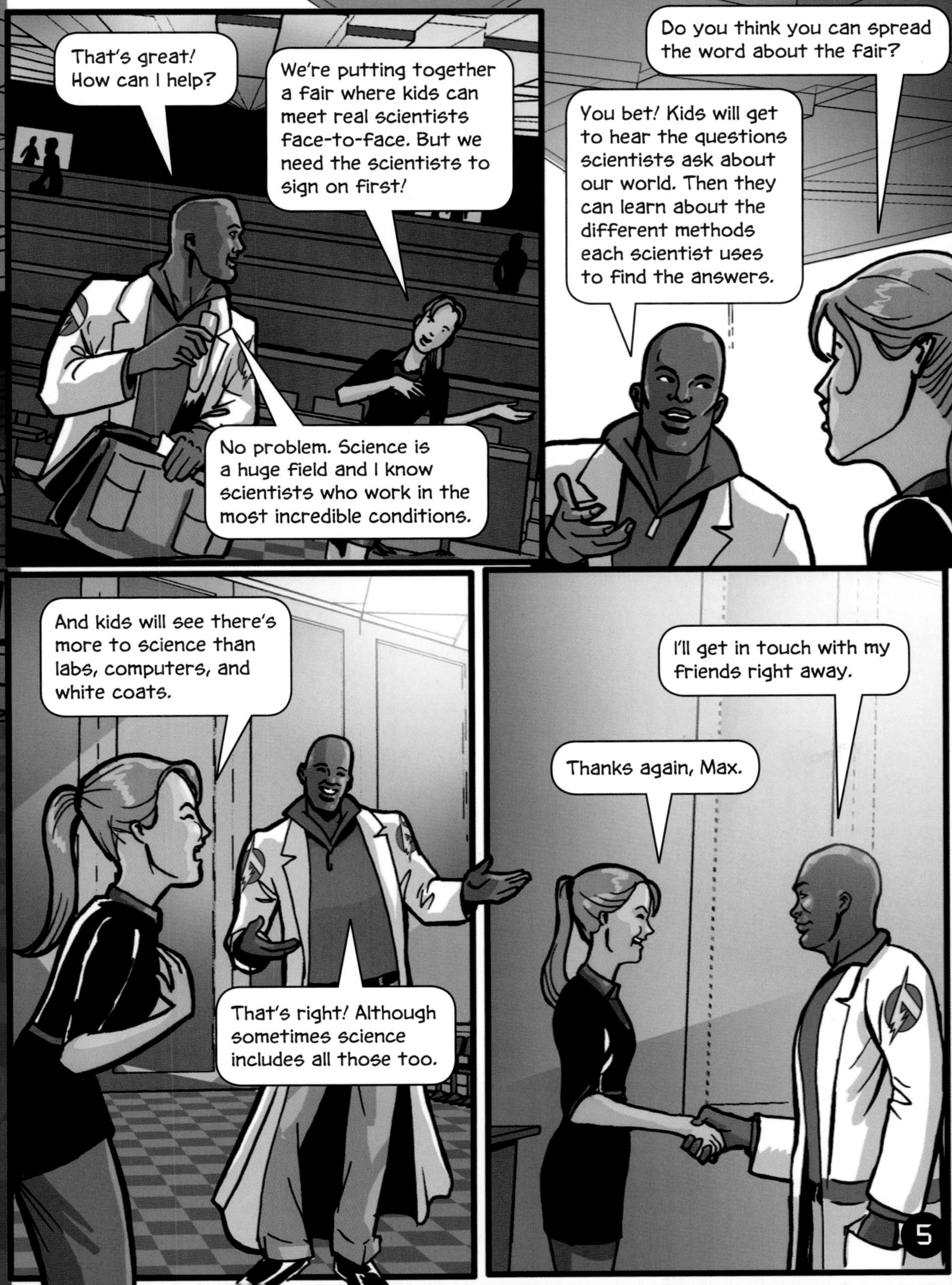
That's great! How can I help?
We're putting together a fair where kids can meet real scientists face-to-face. But we need the scientists to sign on first!
No problem. Science is a huge field and I know scientists who work in the most incredible conditions.
Do you think you can spread the word about the fair?
You bet! Kids will get to hear the questions scientists ask about our world. Then they can learn about the different methods each scientist uses to find the answers.
And kids will see there's more to science than labs, computers, and white coats.
That's right! Although sometimes science includes all those too.
I'll get in touch with my friends right away.
Thanks again, Max.

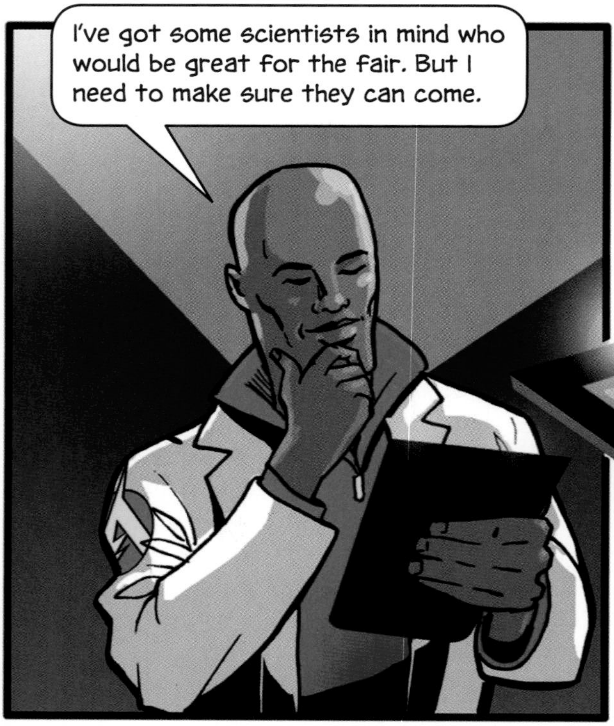
I've got some scientists in mind who would be great for the fair. But I need to make sure they can come.

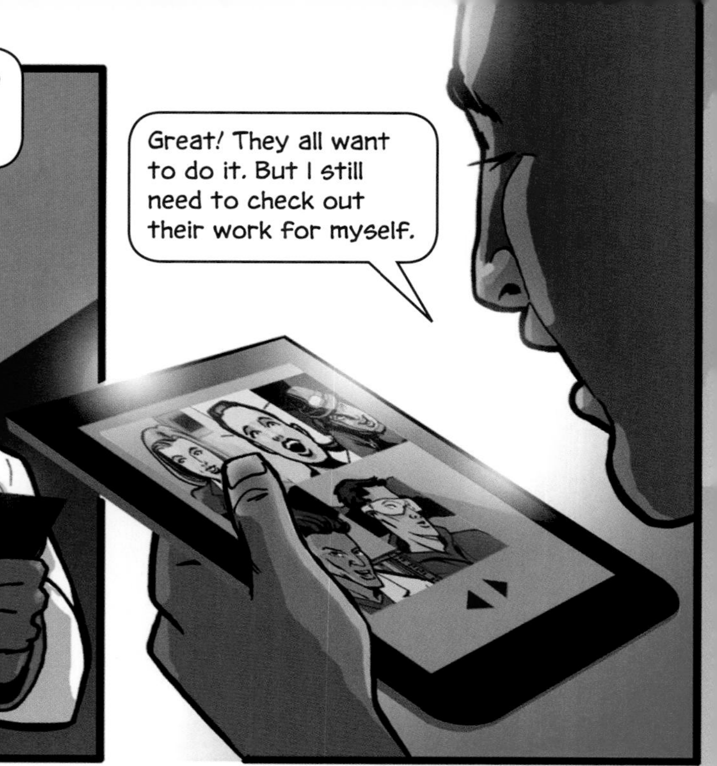
Great! They all want to do it. But I still need to check out their work for myself.

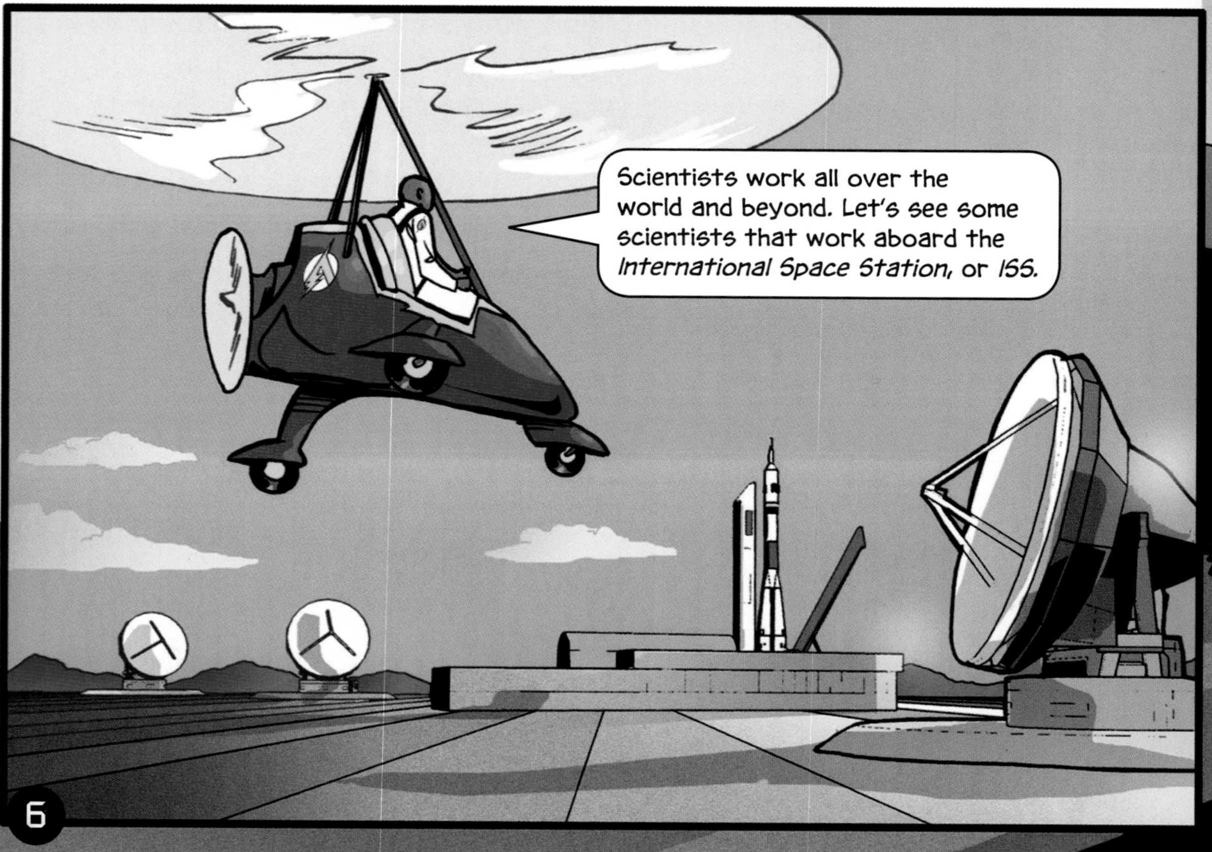
Scientists work all over the world and beyond. Let's see some scientists that work aboard the *International Space Station*, or ISS.

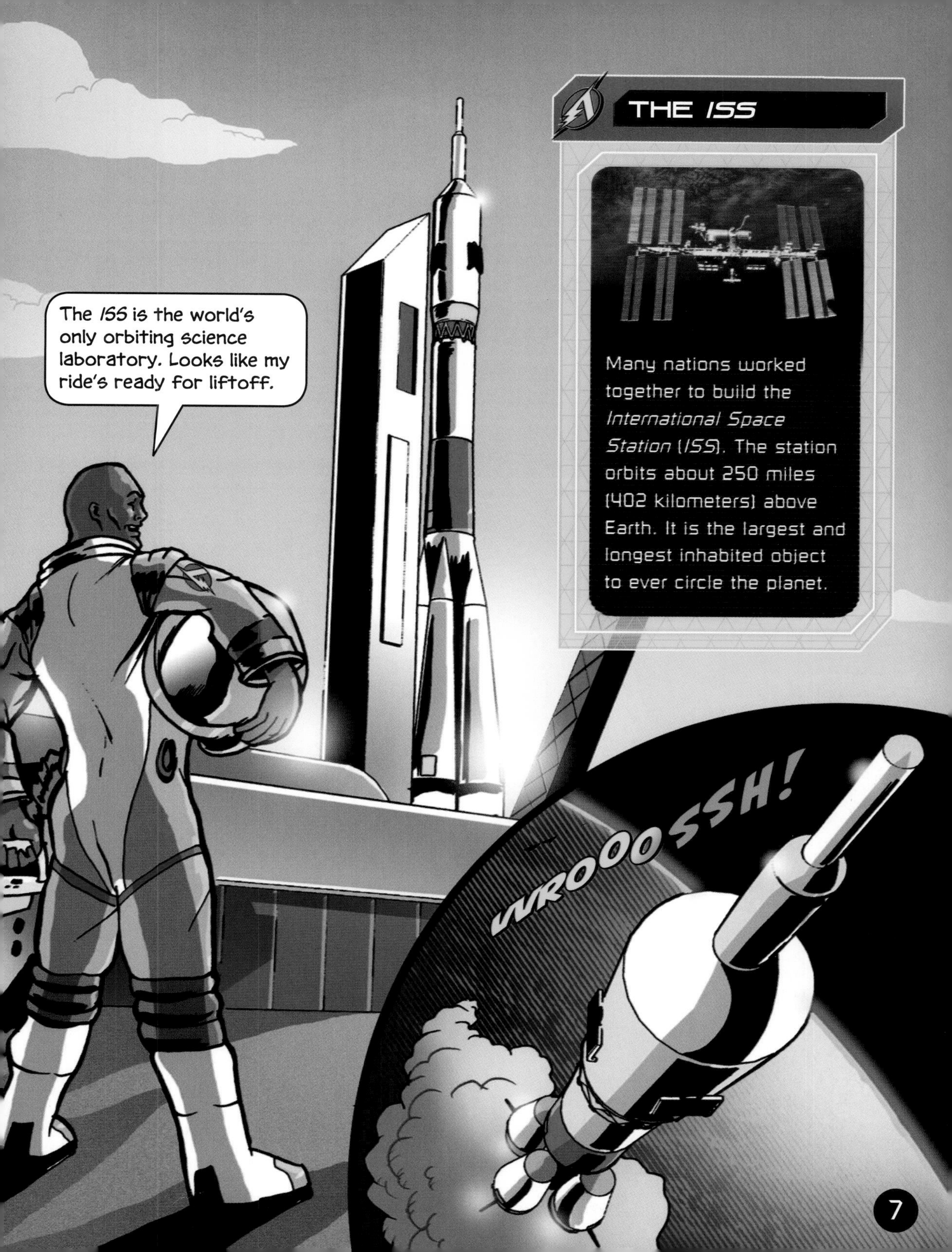
The *ISS* is the world's only orbiting science laboratory. Looks like my ride's ready for liftoff.
THE *ISS*
Many nations worked together to build the *International Space Station* (*ISS*). The station orbits about 250 miles (402 kilometers) above Earth. It is the largest and longest inhabited object to ever circle the planet.
VVROOOOSSH!

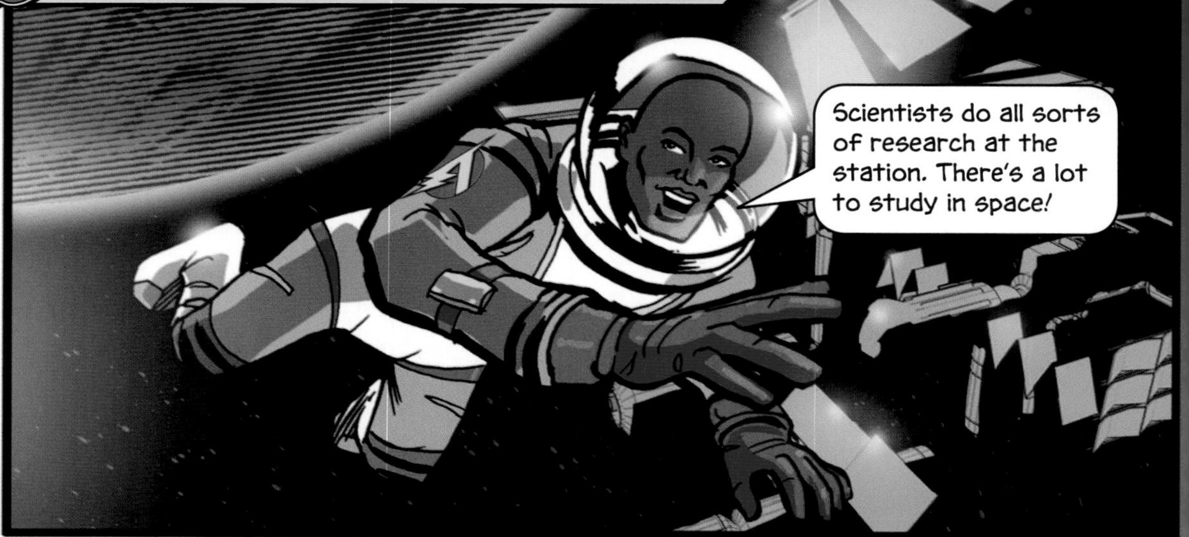
Scientists do all sorts of research at the station. There's a lot to study in space!

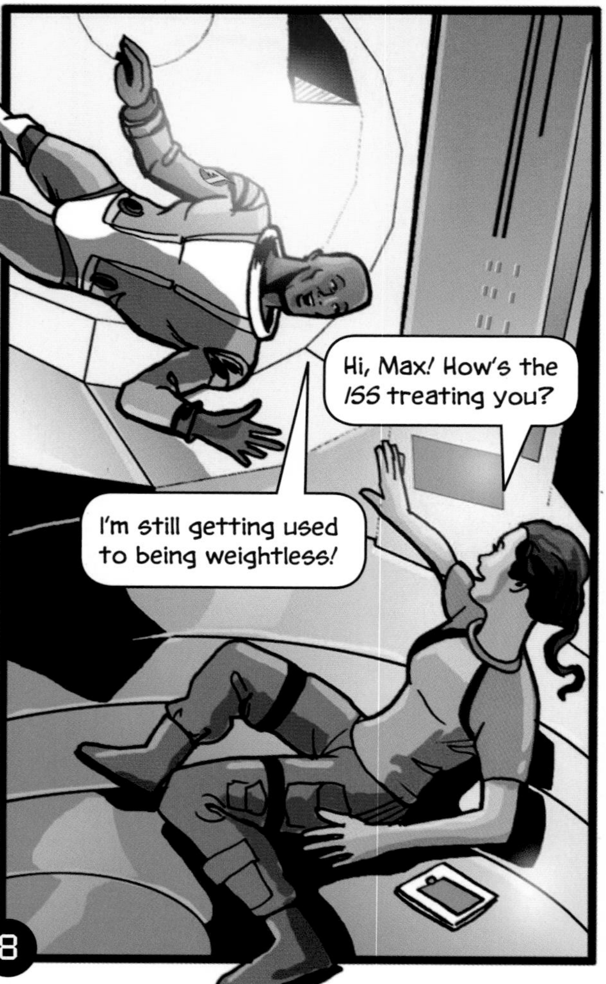
Hi, Max! How's the ISS treating you?
I'm still getting used to being weightless!

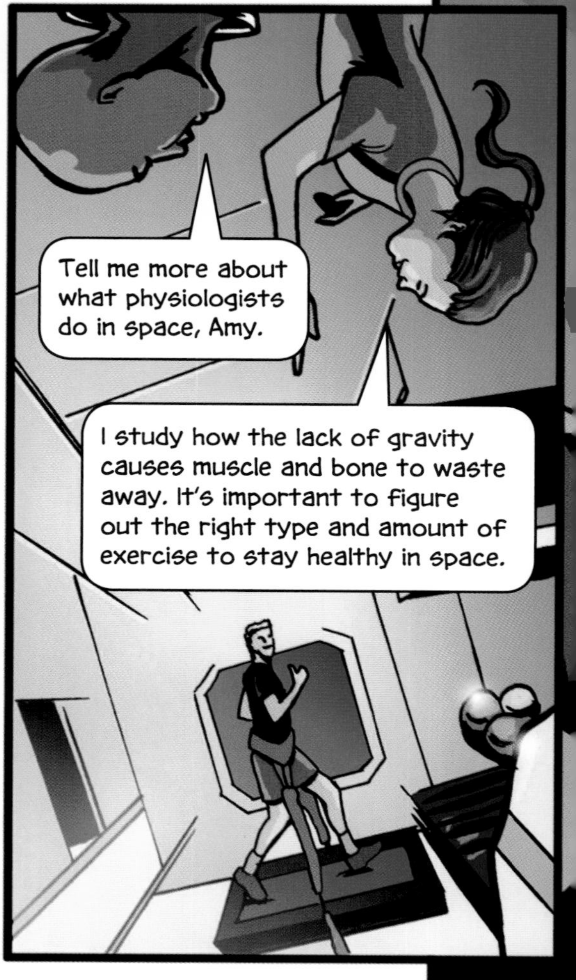
Tell me more about what physiologists do in space, Amy.
I study how the lack of gravity causes muscle and bone to waste away. It's important to figure out the right type and amount of exercise to stay healthy in space.

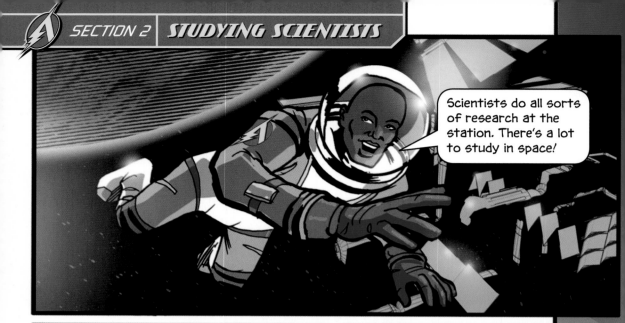

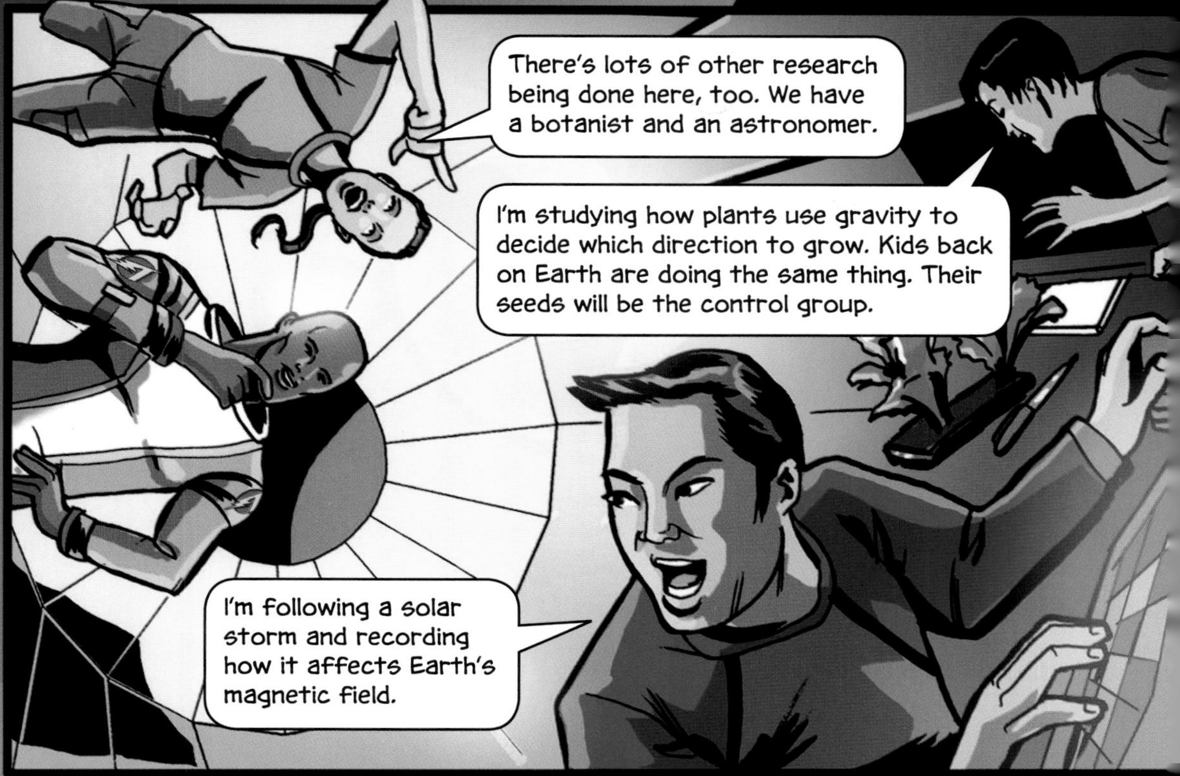
There's lots of other research being done here, too. We have a botanist and an astronomer.
I'm studying how plants use gravity to decide which direction to grow. Kids back on Earth are doing the same thing. Their seeds will be the control group.
I'm following a solar storm and recording how it affects Earth's magnetic field.

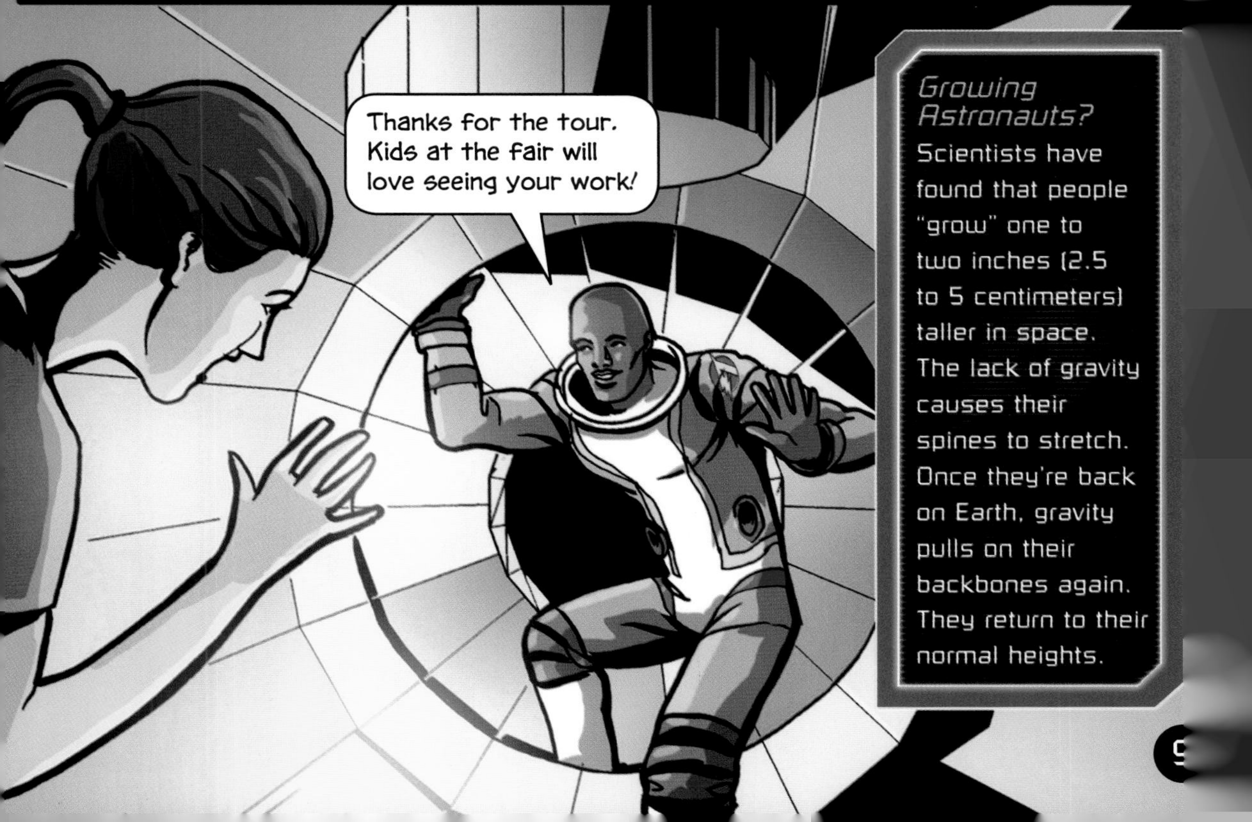
Thanks for the tour. Kids at the fair will love seeing your work!

Growing Astronauts?

Scientists have found that people "grow" one to two inches (2.5 to 5 centimeters) taller in space. The lack of gravity causes their spines to stretch. Once they're back on Earth, gravity pulls on their backbones again. They return to their normal heights.

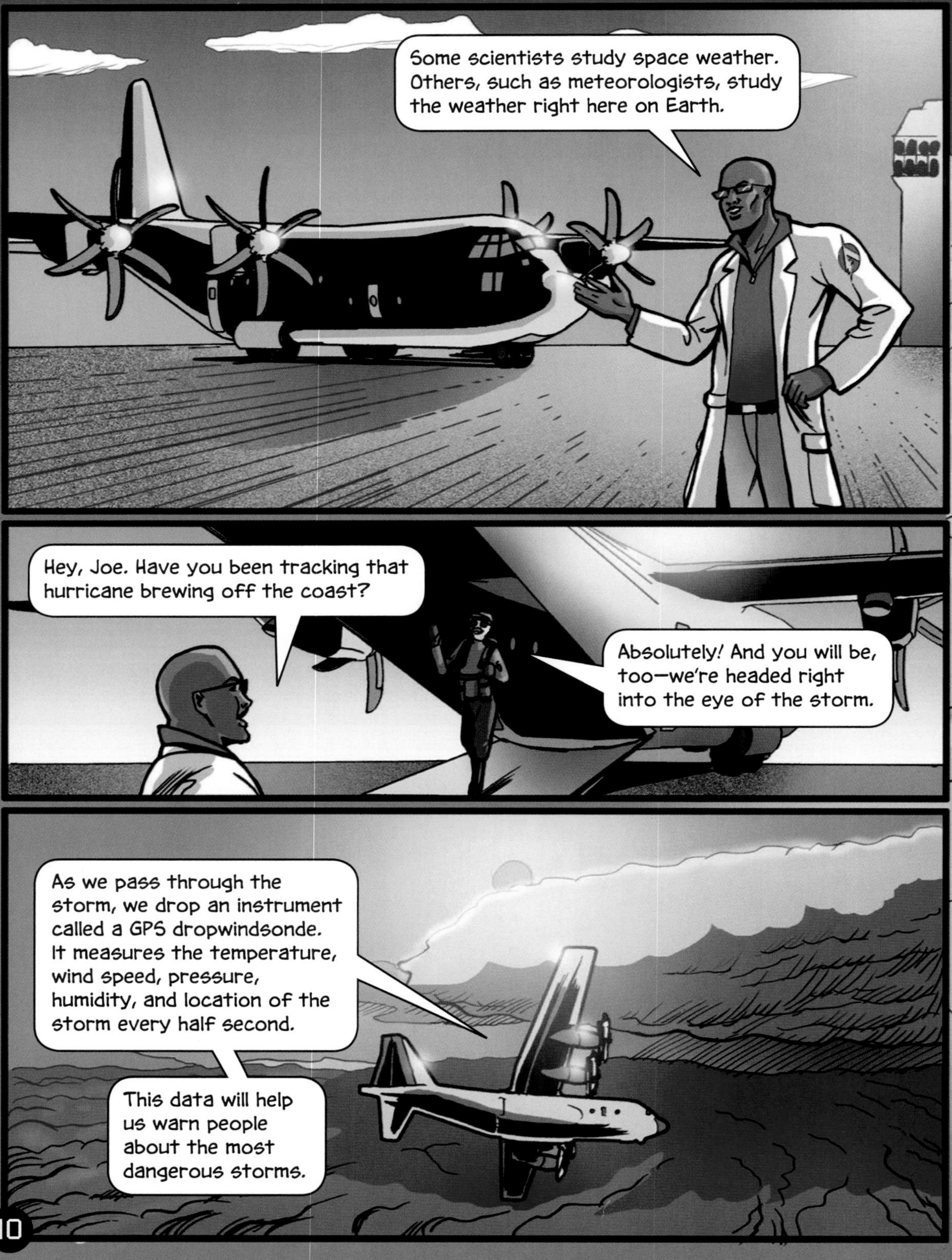
Some scientists study space weather. Others, such as meteorologists, study the weather right here on Earth.
Hey, Joe. Have you been tracking that hurricane brewing off the coast?
Absolutely! And you will be, too—we're headed right into the eye of the storm.
As we pass through the storm, we drop an instrument called a GPS dropwindsonde. It measures the temperature, wind speed, pressure, humidity, and location of the storm every half second.
This data will help us warn people about the most dangerous storms.

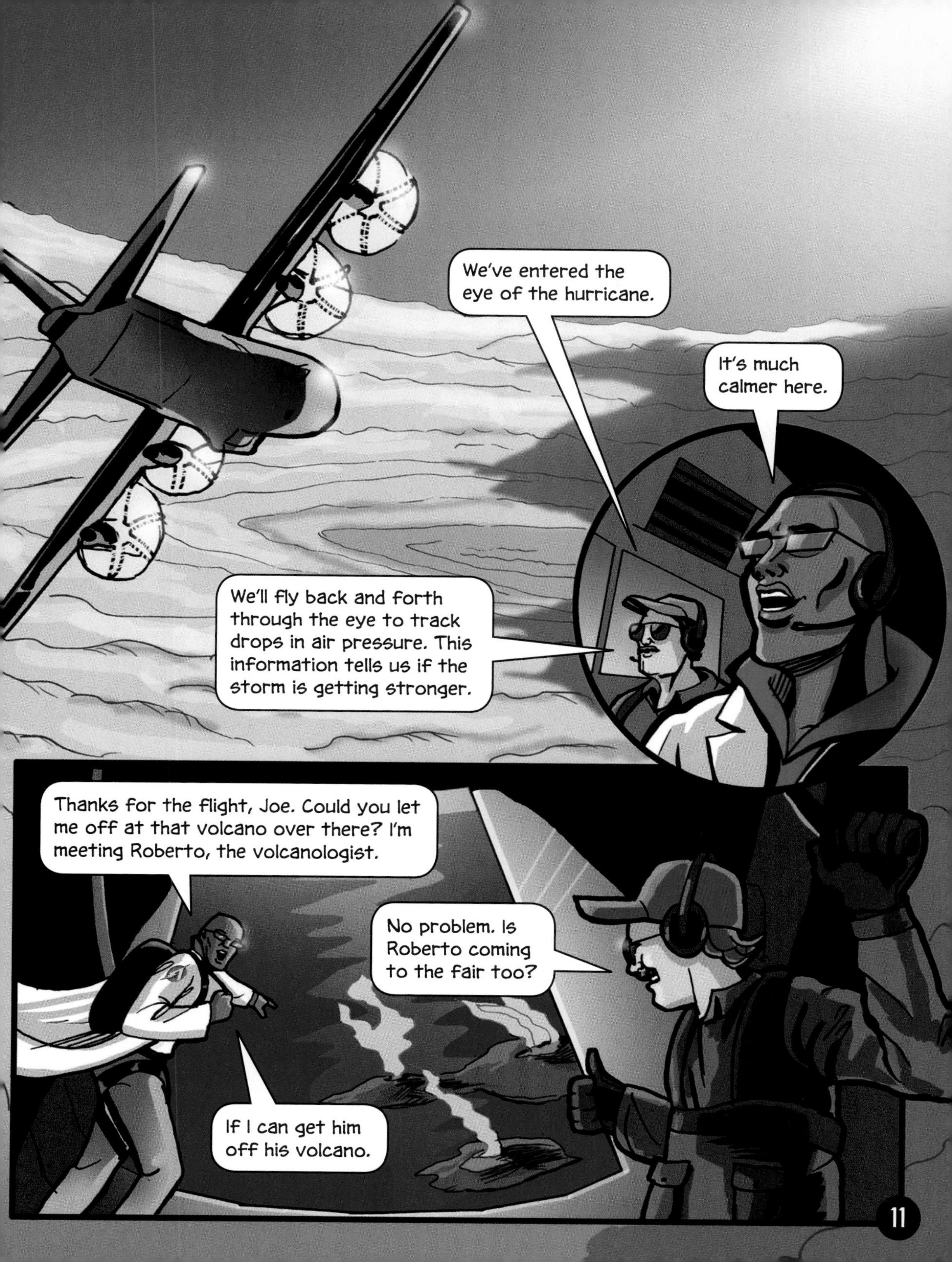
We've entered the eye of the hurricane.
It's much calmer here.
We'll fly back and forth through the eye to track drops in air pressure. This information tells us if the storm is getting stronger.
Thanks for the flight, Joe. Could you let me off at that volcano over there? I'm meeting Roberto, the volcanologist.
No problem. Is Roberto coming to the fair too?
If I can get him off his volcano.

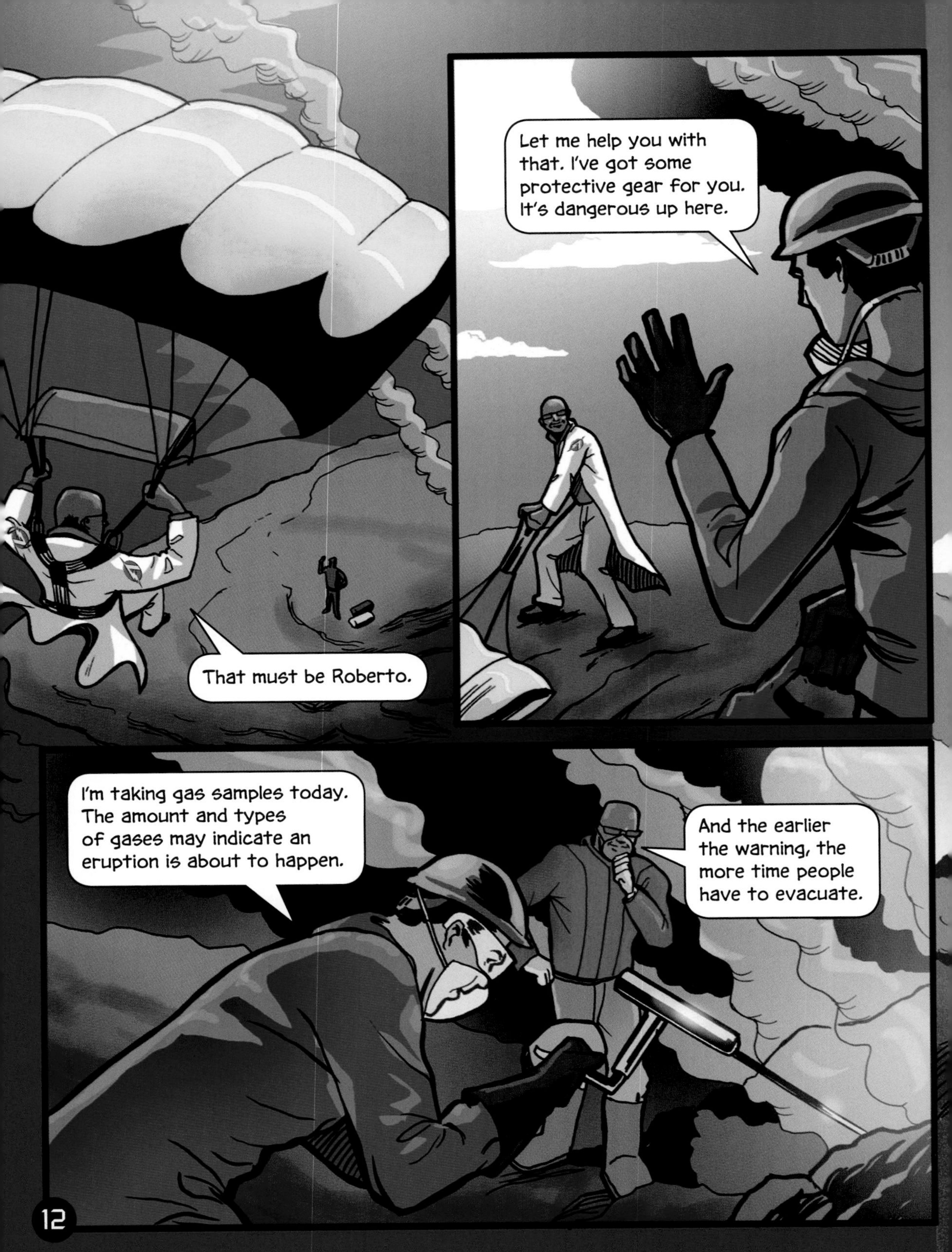
That must be Roberto.
Let me help you with that. I've got some protective gear for you. It's dangerous up here.
I'm taking gas samples today. The amount and types of gases may indicate an eruption is about to happen.
And the earlier the warning, the more time people have to evacuate.

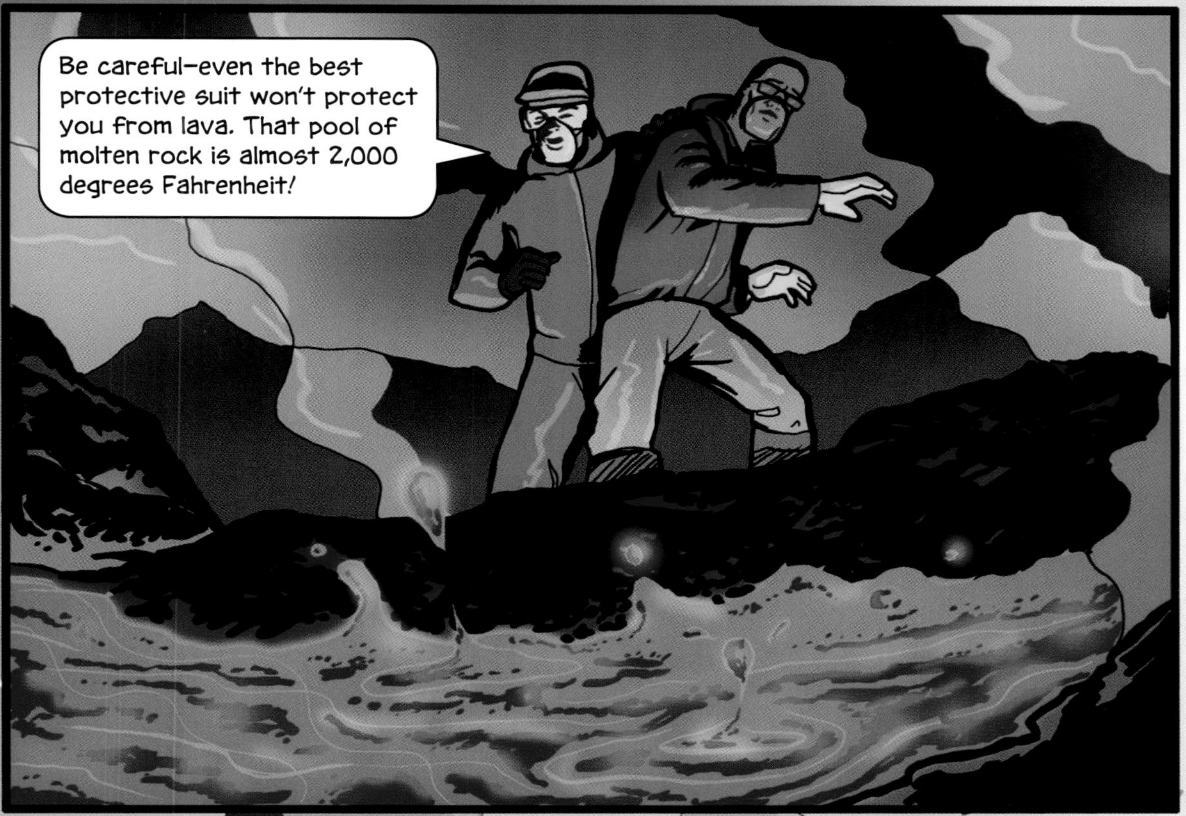
Be careful—even the best protective suit won't protect you from lava. That pool of molten rock is almost 2,000 degrees Fahrenheit!

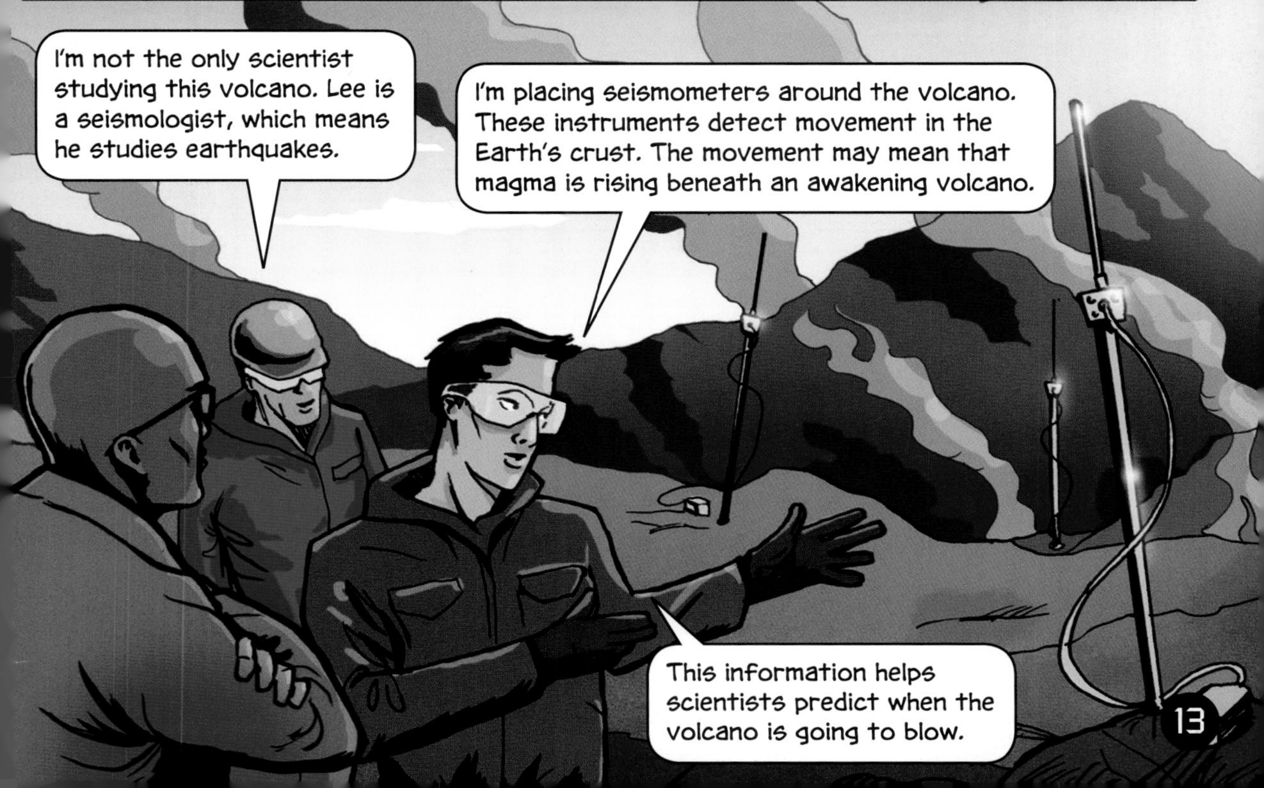
I'm not the only scientist studying this volcano. Lee is a seismologist, which means he studies earthquakes.
I'm placing seismometers around the volcano. These instruments detect movement in the Earth's crust. The movement may mean that magma is rising beneath an awakening volcano.
This information helps scientists predict when the volcano is going to blow.

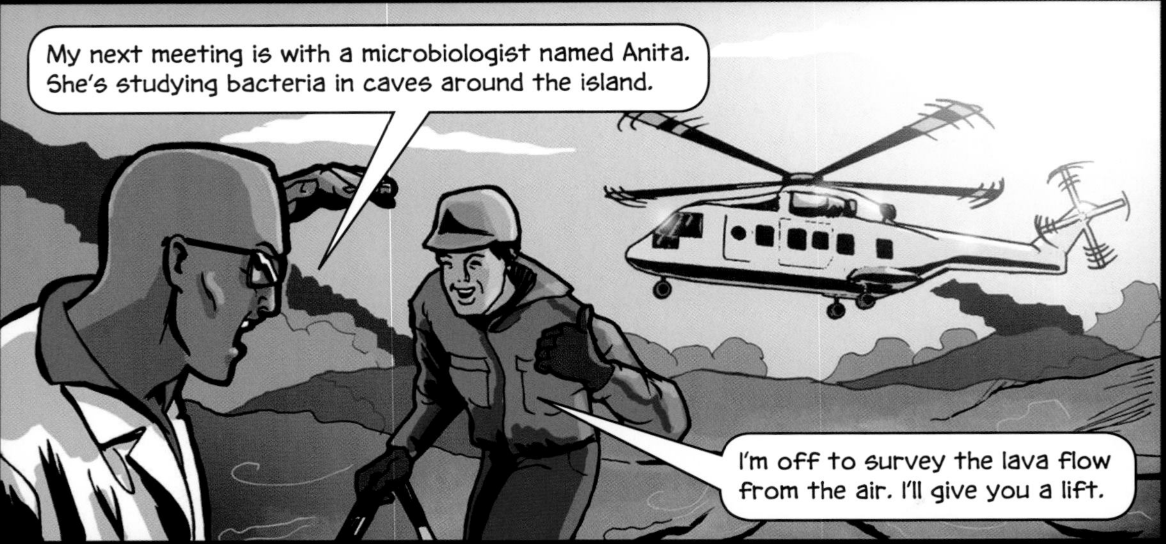
My next meeting is with a microbiologist named Anita. She's studying bacteria in caves around the island.
I'm off to survey the lava flow from the air. I'll give you a lift.

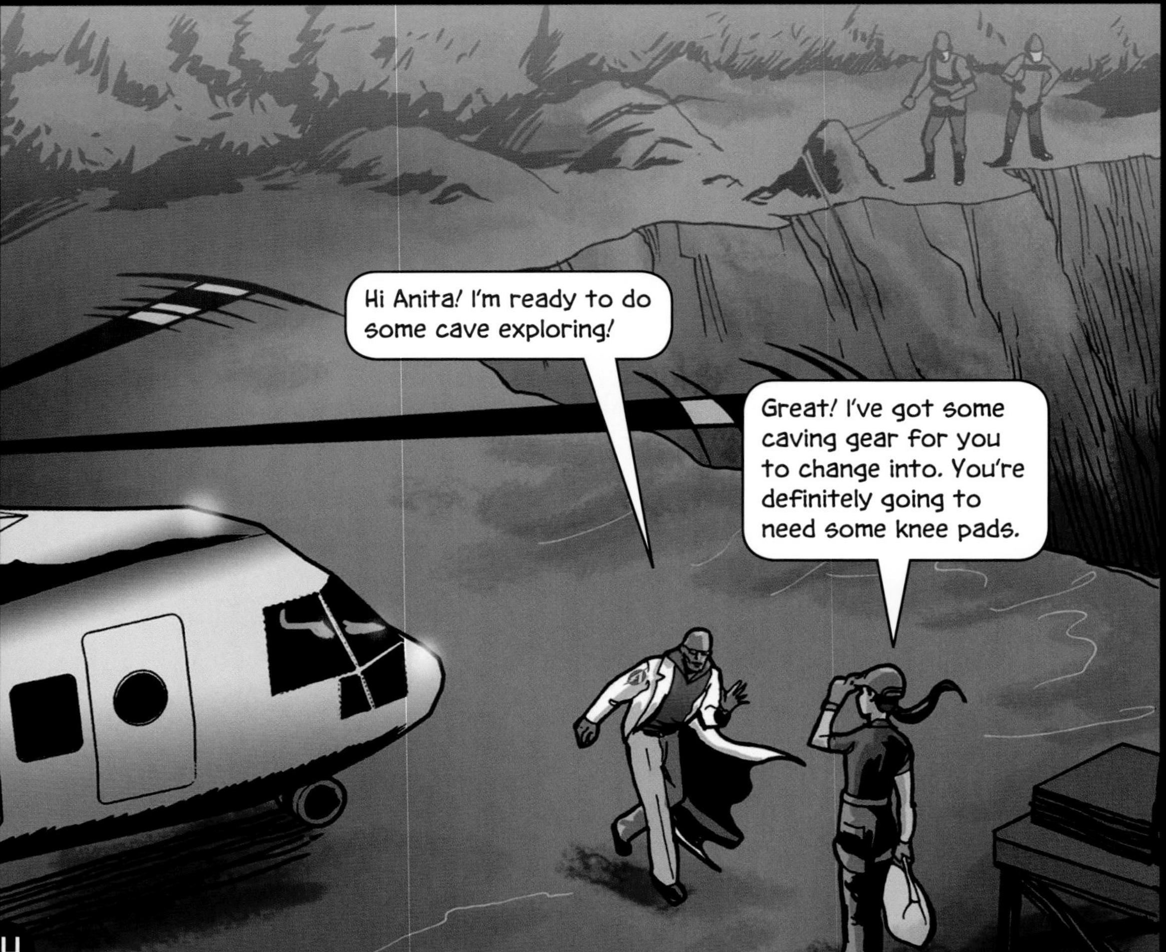
Hi Anita! I'm ready to do some cave exploring!
Great! I've got some caving gear for you to change into. You're definitely going to need some knee pads.

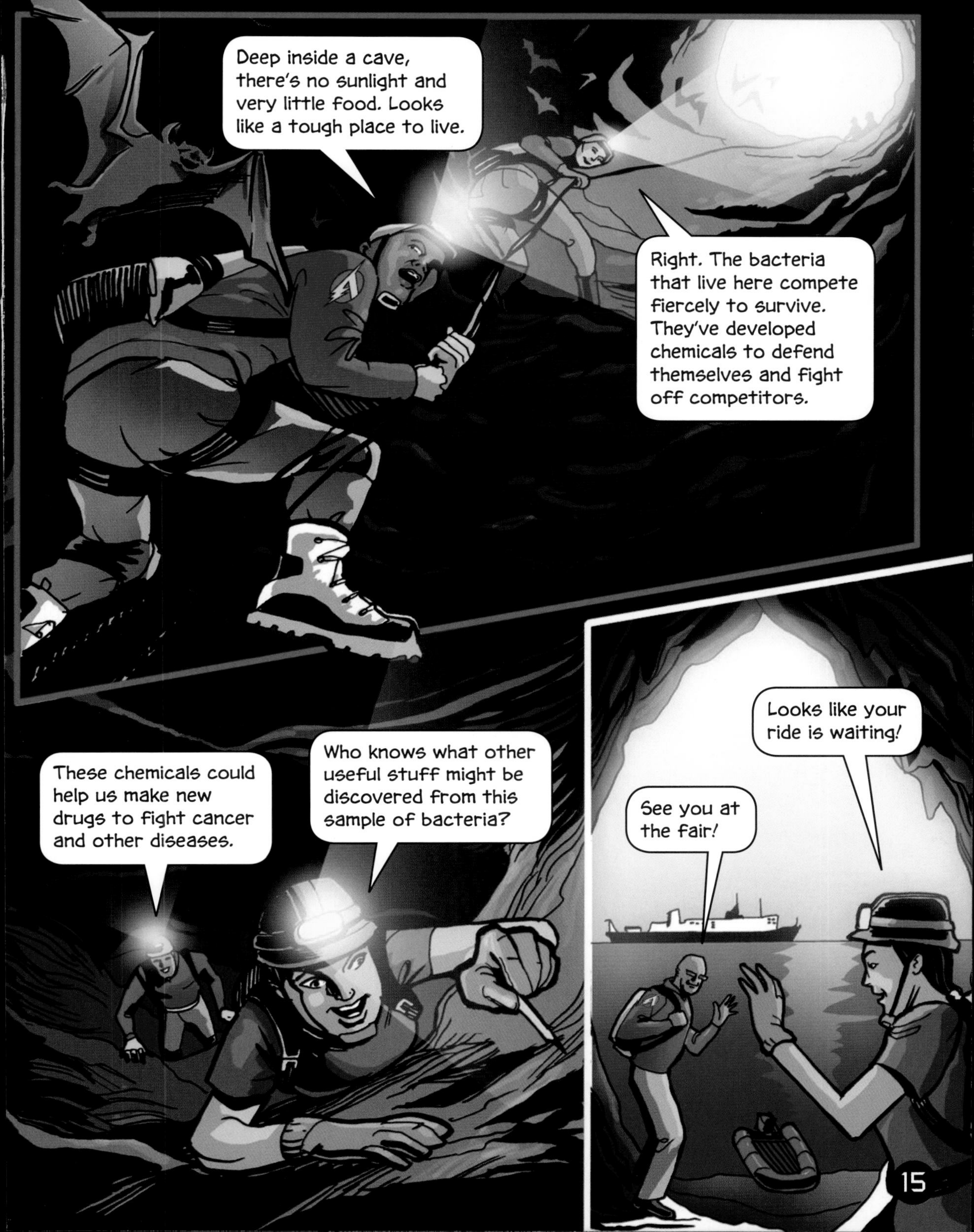
Deep inside a cave, there's no sunlight and very little food. Looks like a tough place to live.
Right. The bacteria that live here compete fiercely to survive. They've developed chemicals to defend themselves and fight off competitors.
These chemicals could help us make new drugs to fight cancer and other diseases.
Who knows what other useful stuff might be discovered from this sample of bacteria?
See you at the fair!
Looks like your ride is waiting!

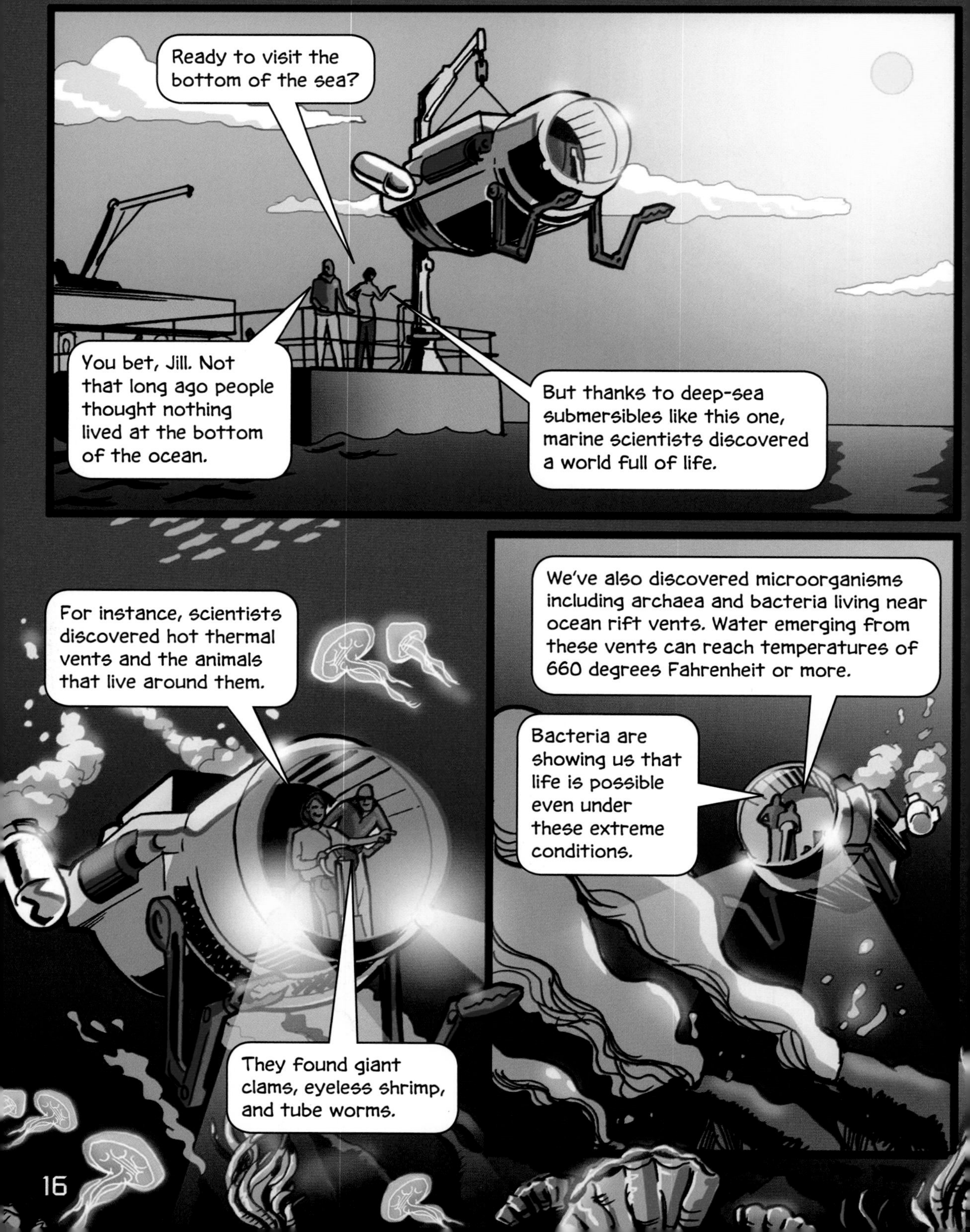
Ready to visit the bottom of the sea?
You bet, Jill. Not that long ago people thought nothing lived at the bottom of the ocean.
But thanks to deep-sea submersibles like this one, marine scientists discovered a world full of life.
For instance, scientists discovered hot thermal vents and the animals that live around them.
They found giant clams, eyeless shrimp, and tube worms.
We've also discovered microorganisms including archaea and bacteria living near ocean rift vents. Water emerging from these vents can reach temperatures of 660 degrees Fahrenheit or more.
Bacteria are showing us that life is possible even under these extreme conditions.

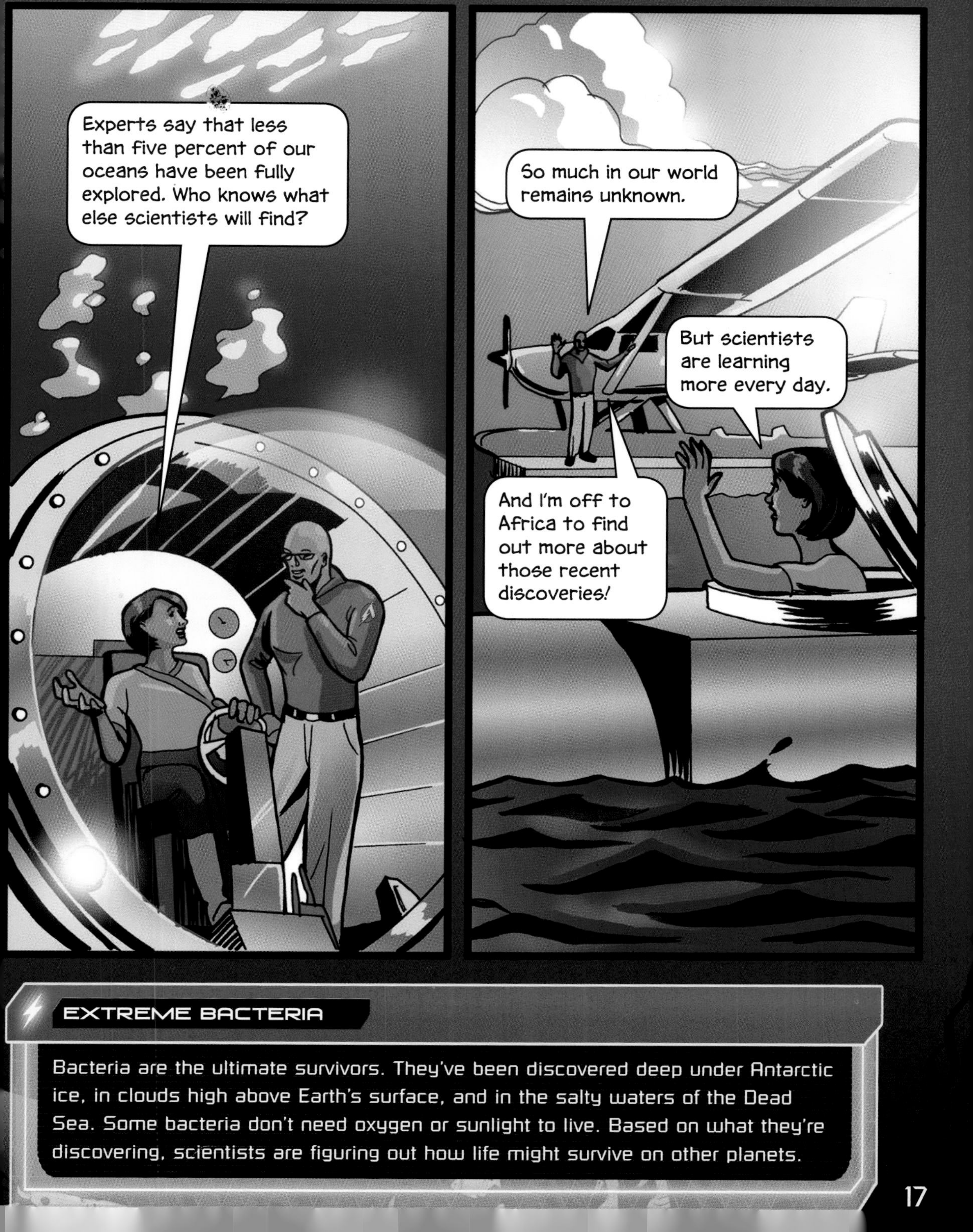
Experts say that less than five percent of our oceans have been fully explored. Who knows what else scientists will find?
So much in our world remains unknown.
But scientists are learning more every day.
And I'm off to Africa to find out more about those recent discoveries!

EXTREME BACTERIA

Bacteria are the ultimate survivors. They've been discovered deep under Antarctic ice, in clouds high above Earth's surface, and in the salty waters of the Dead Sea. Some bacteria don't need oxygen or sunlight to live. Based on what they're discovering, scientists are figuring out how life might survive on other planets.

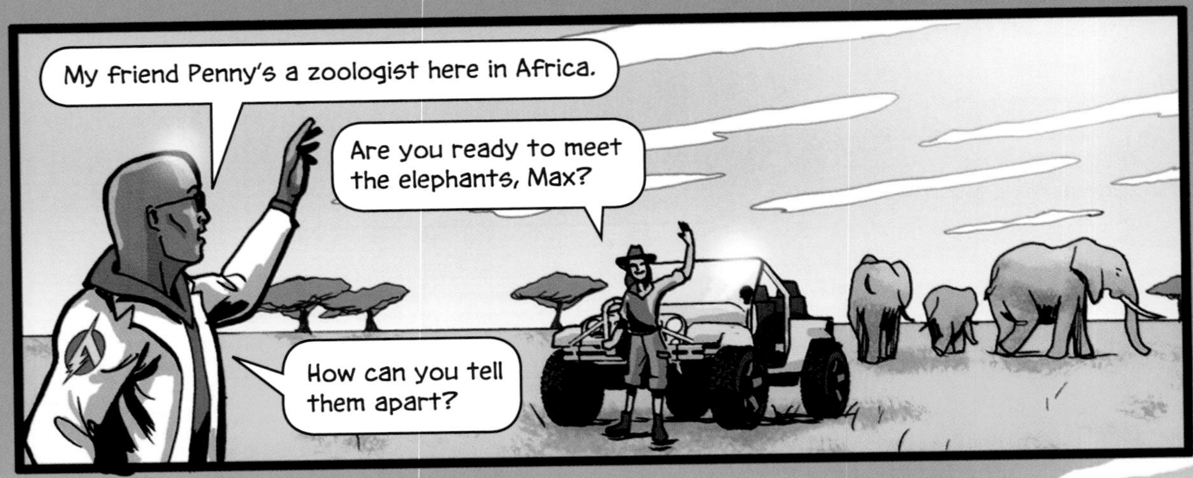
My friend Penny's a zoologist here in Africa.
Are you ready to meet the elephants, Max?
How can you tell them apart?

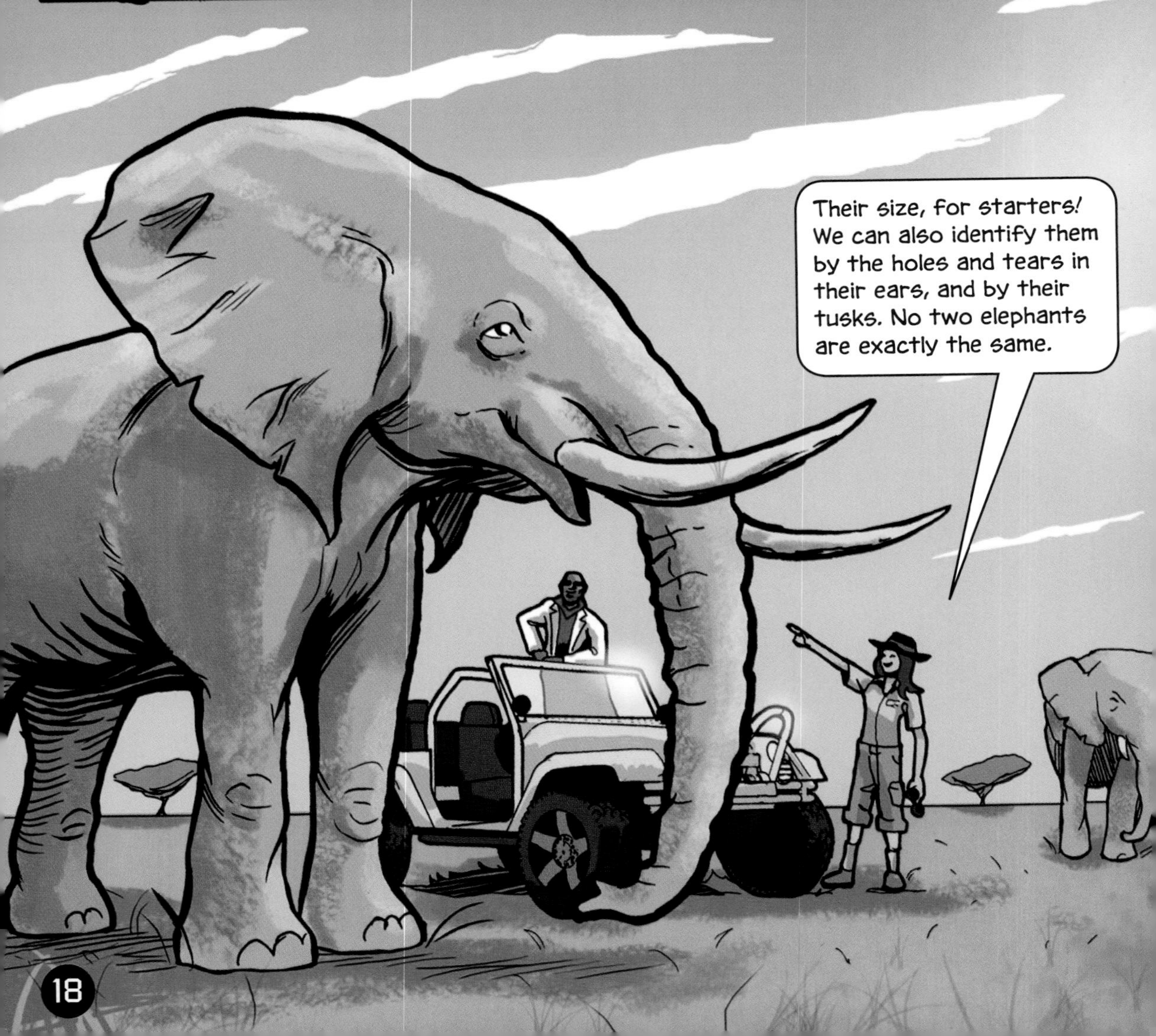
Their size, for starters! We can also identify them by the holes and tears in their ears, and by their tusks. No two elephants are exactly the same.

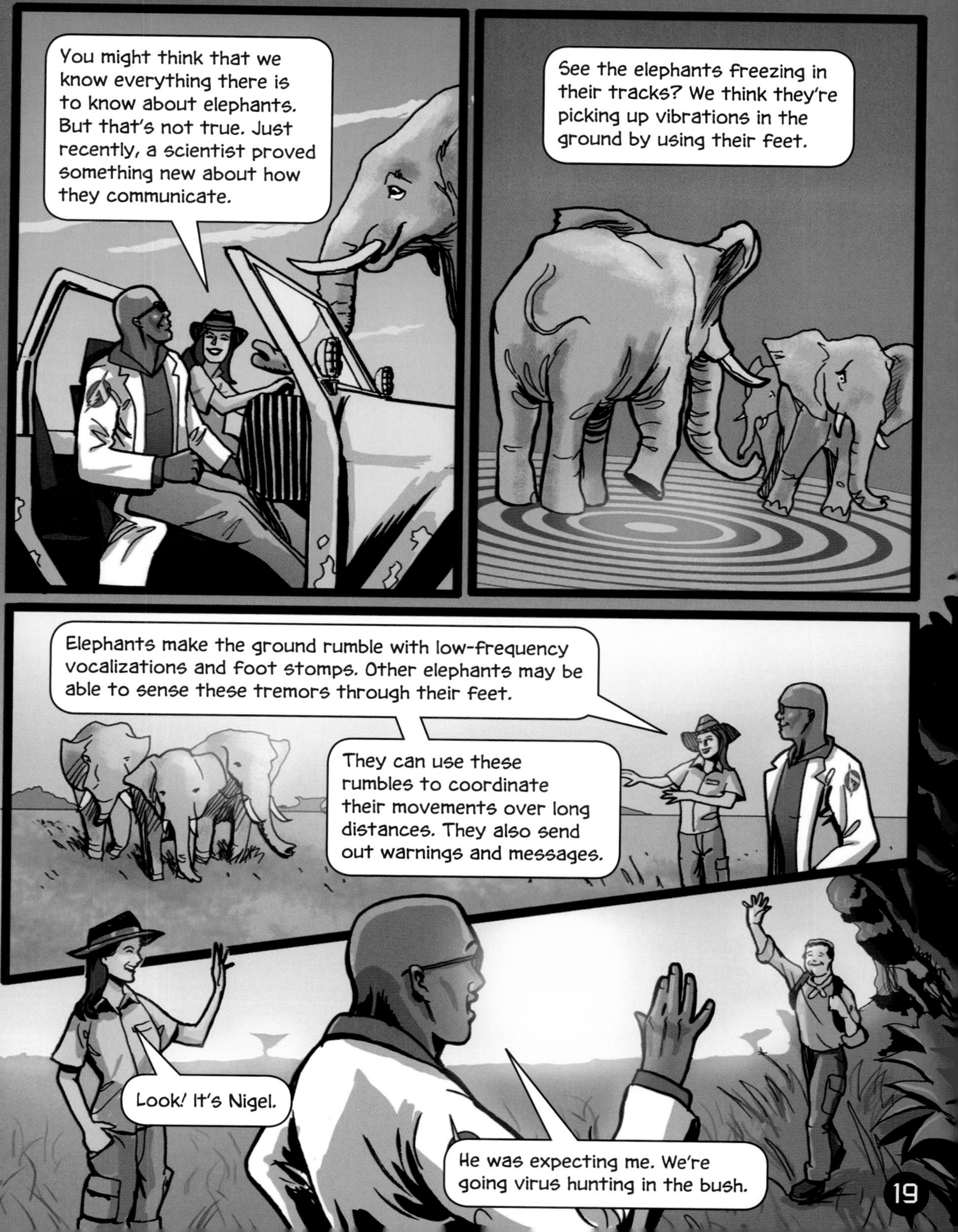

You might think that we know everything there is to know about elephants. But that's not true. Just recently, a scientist proved something new about how they communicate.
See the elephants freezing in their tracks? We think they're picking up vibrations in the ground by using their feet.
Elephants make the ground rumble with low-frequency vocalizations and foot stomps. Other elephants may be able to sense these tremors through their feet.
They can use these rumbles to coordinate their movements over long distances. They also send out warnings and messages.
Look! It's Nigel.
He was expecting me. We're going virus hunting in the bush.

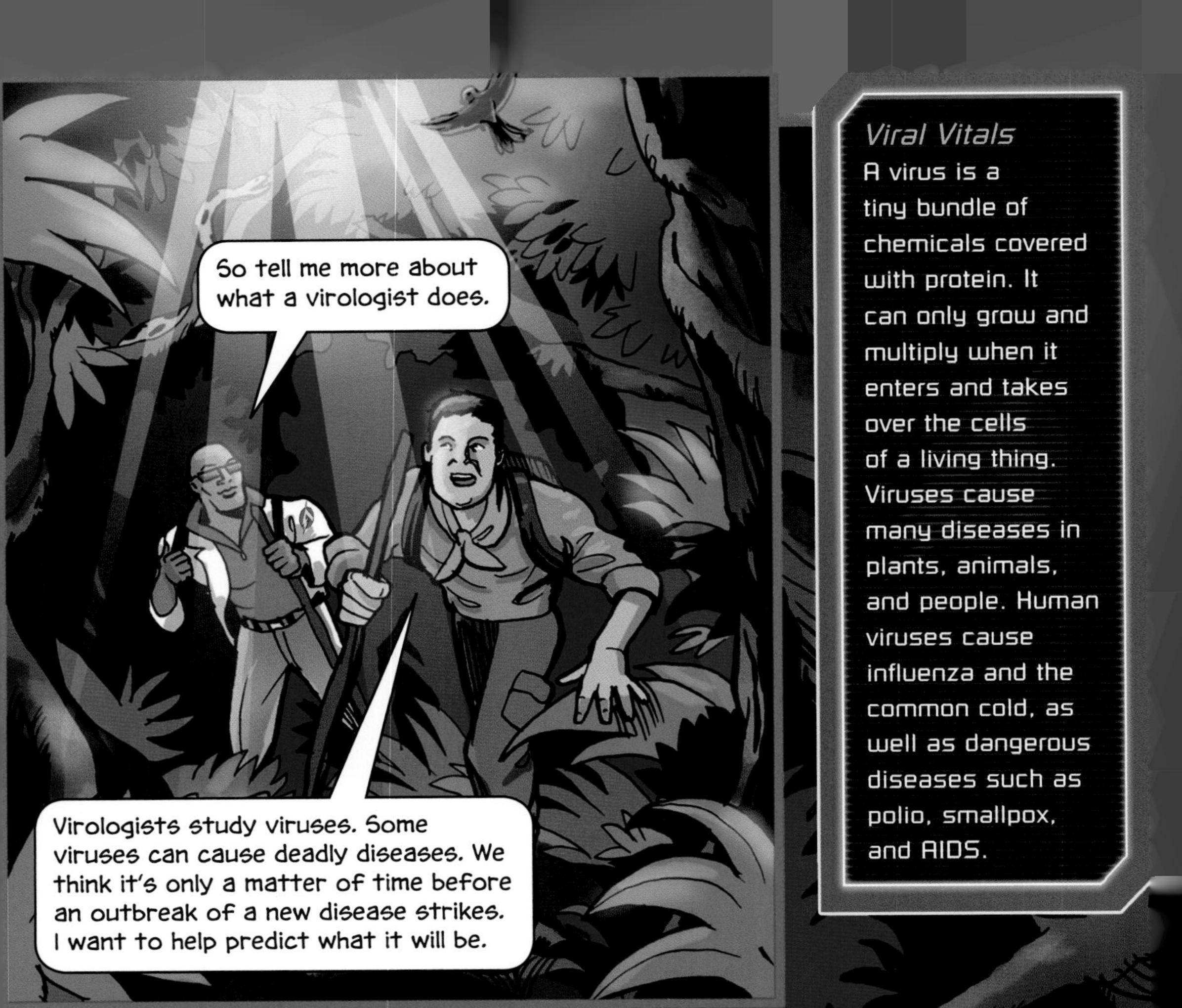
So tell me more about what a virologist does.
Virologists study viruses. Some viruses can cause deadly diseases. We think it's only a matter of time before an outbreak of a new disease strikes. I want to help predict what it will be.

Viral Vitals

A virus is a tiny bundle of chemicals covered with protein. It can only grow and multiply when it enters and takes over the cells of a living thing. Viruses cause many diseases in plants, animals, and people. Human viruses cause influenza and the common cold, as well as dangerous diseases such as polio, smallpox, and AIDS.

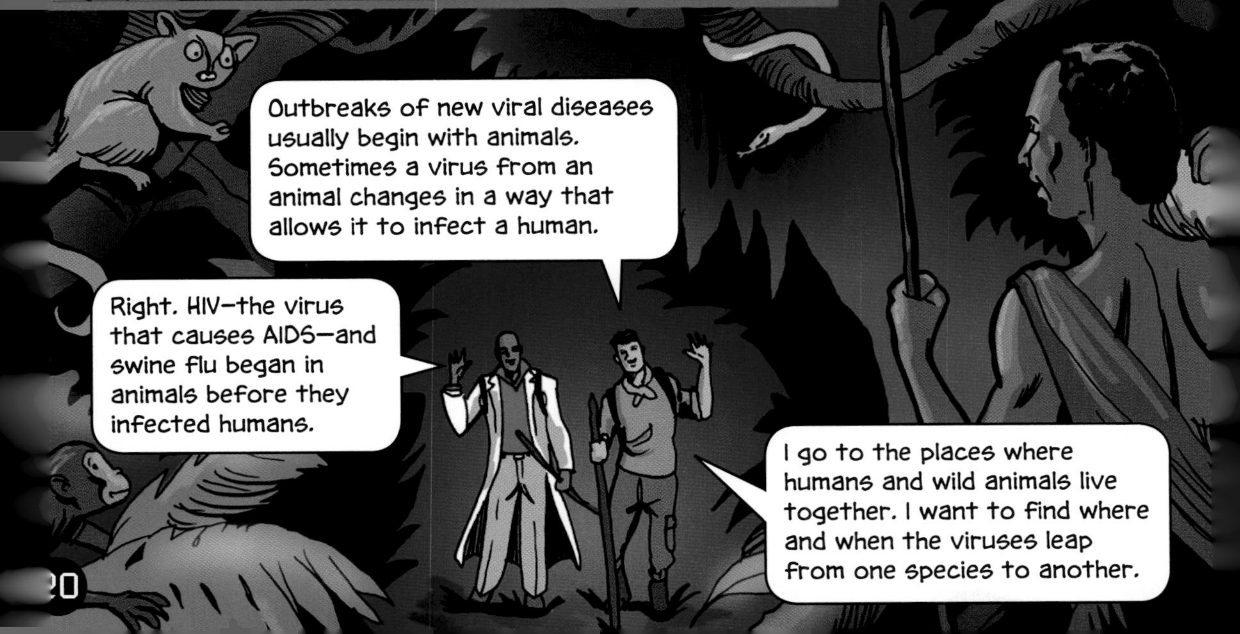
Outbreaks of new viral diseases usually begin with animals. Sometimes a virus from an animal changes in a way that allows it to infect a human.
Right. HIV—the virus that causes AIDS—and swine flu began in animals before they infected humans.
I go to the places where humans and wild animals live together. I want to find where and when the viruses leap from one species to another.

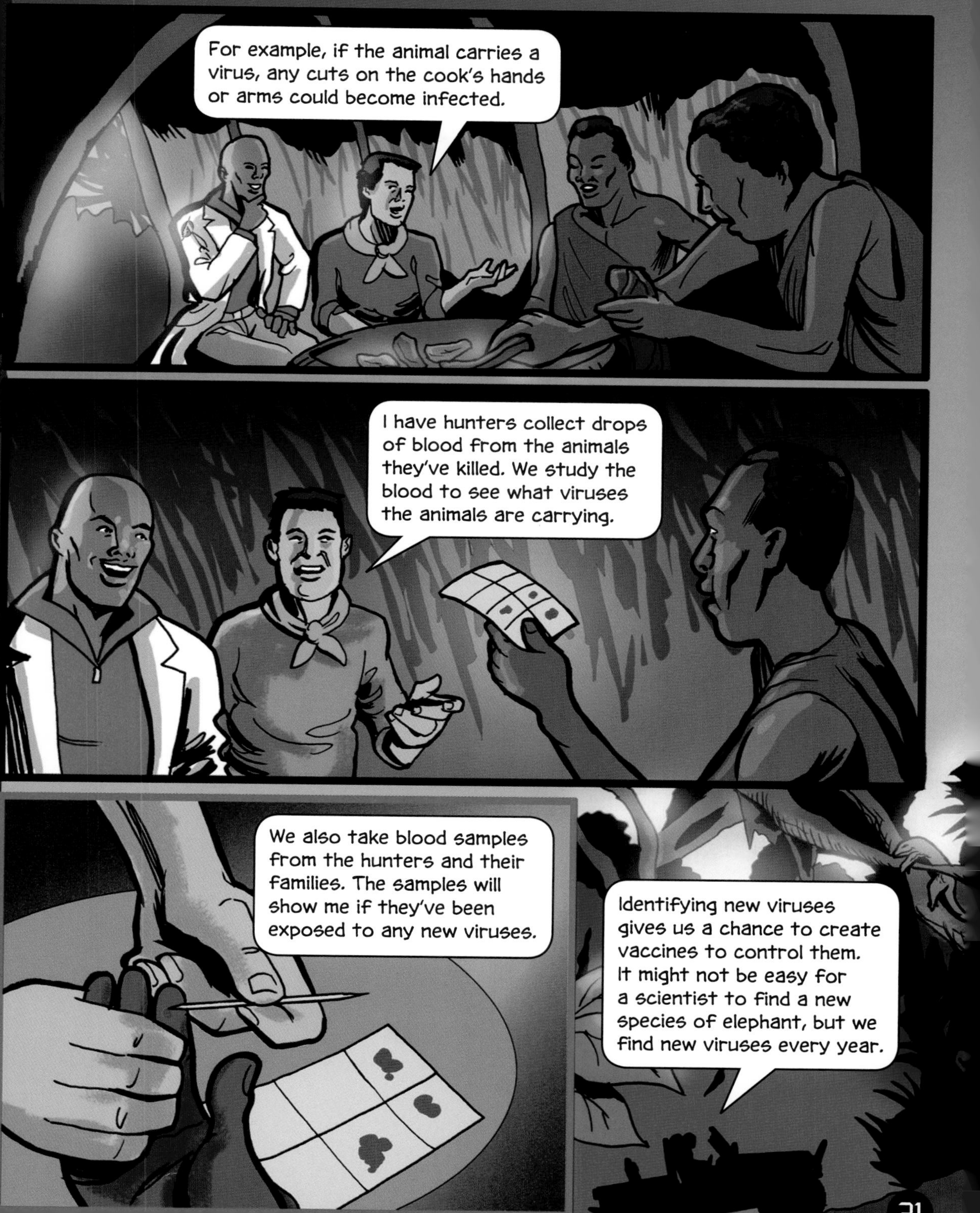
For example, if the animal carries a virus, any cuts on the cook's hands or arms could become infected.
I have hunters collect drops of blood from the animals they've killed. We study the blood to see what viruses the animals are carrying.
We also take blood samples from the hunters and their families. The samples will show me if they've been exposed to any new viruses.
Identifying new viruses gives us a chance to create vaccines to control them. It might not be easy for a scientist to find a new species of elephant, but we find new viruses every year.

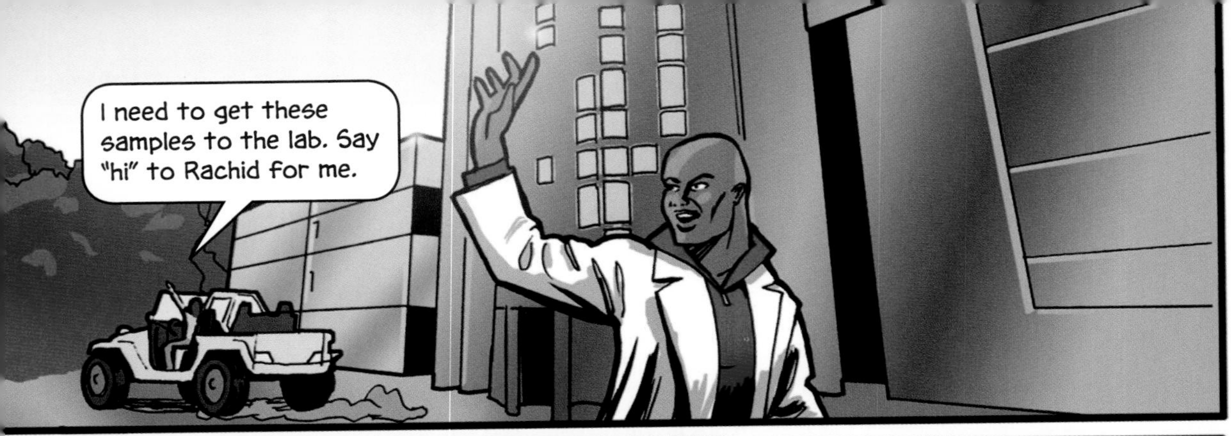
I need to get these samples to the lab. Say "hi" to Rachid for me.

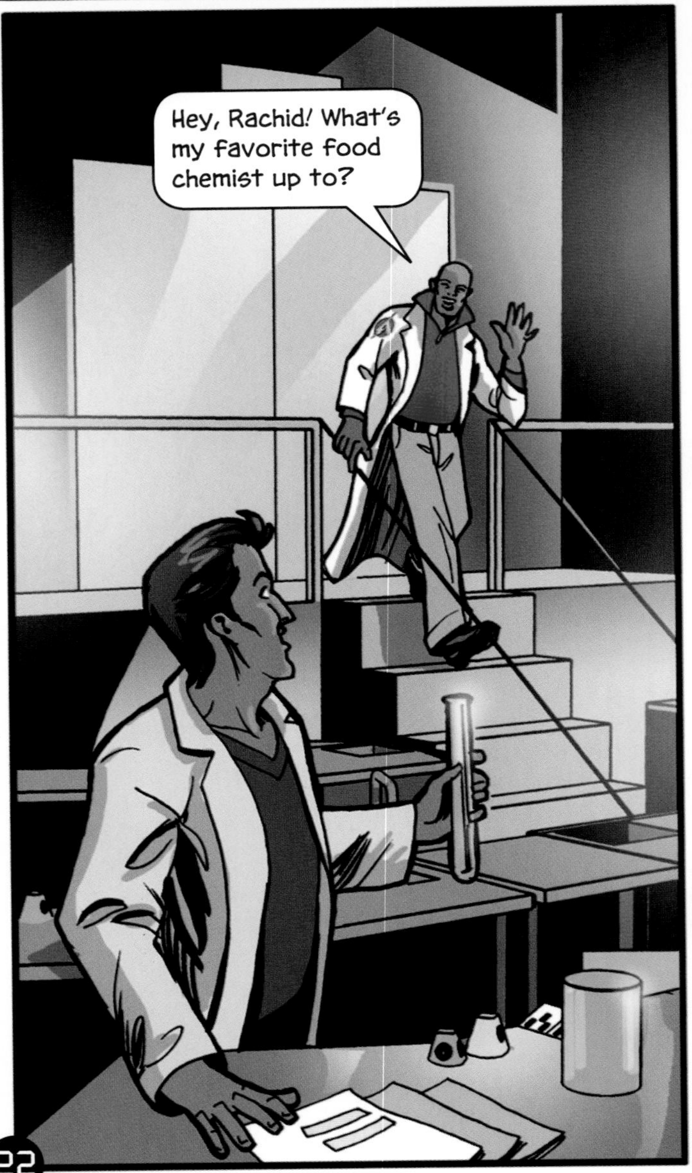
Hey, Rachid! What's my favorite food chemist up to?

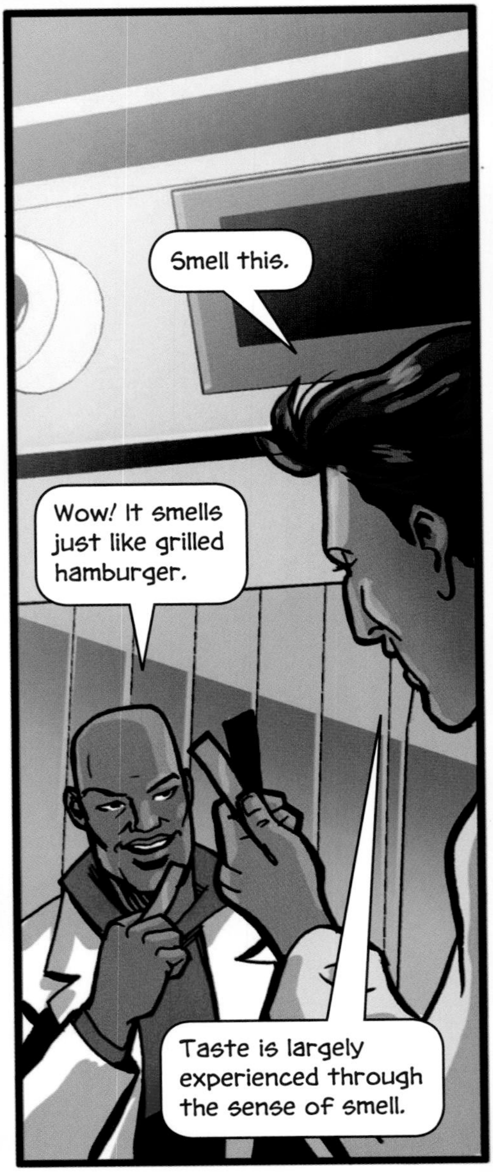
Smell this.
Wow! It smells just like grilled hamburger.
Taste is largely experienced through the sense of smell.

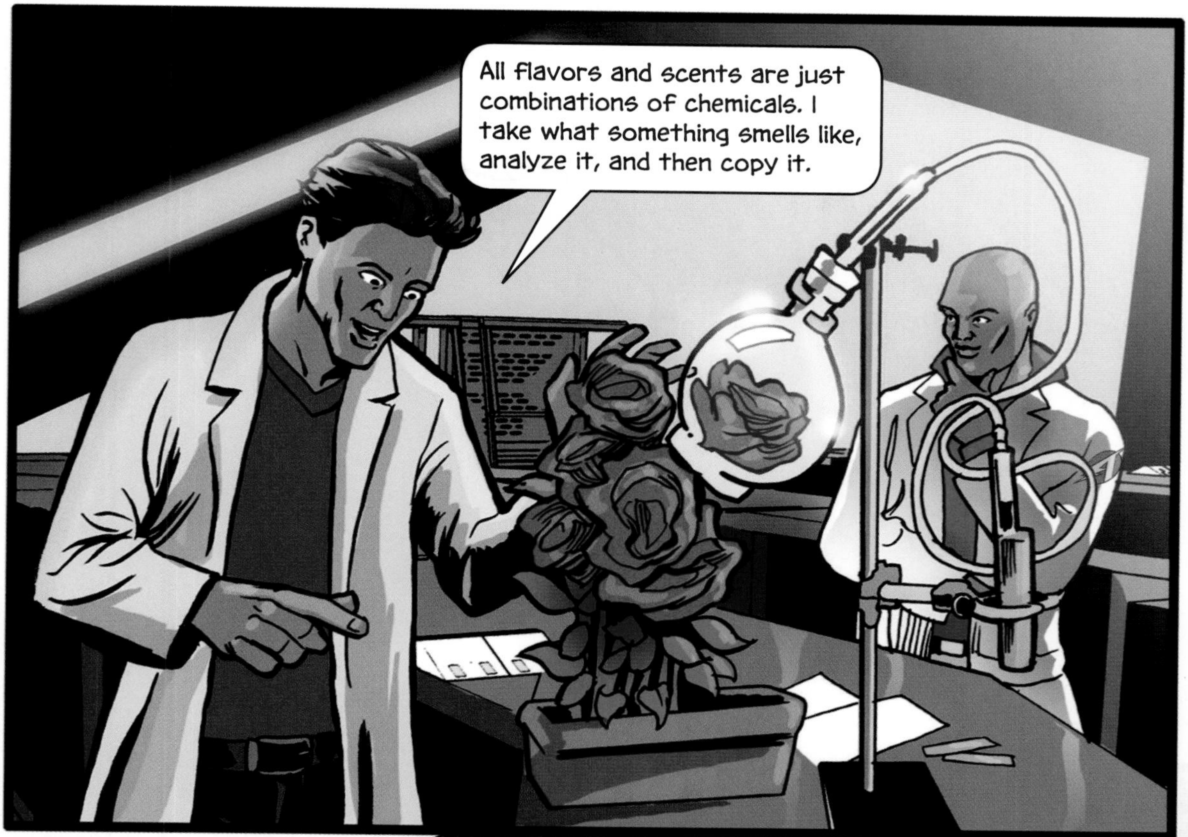
All flavors and scents are just combinations of chemicals. I take what something smells like, analyze it, and then copy it.

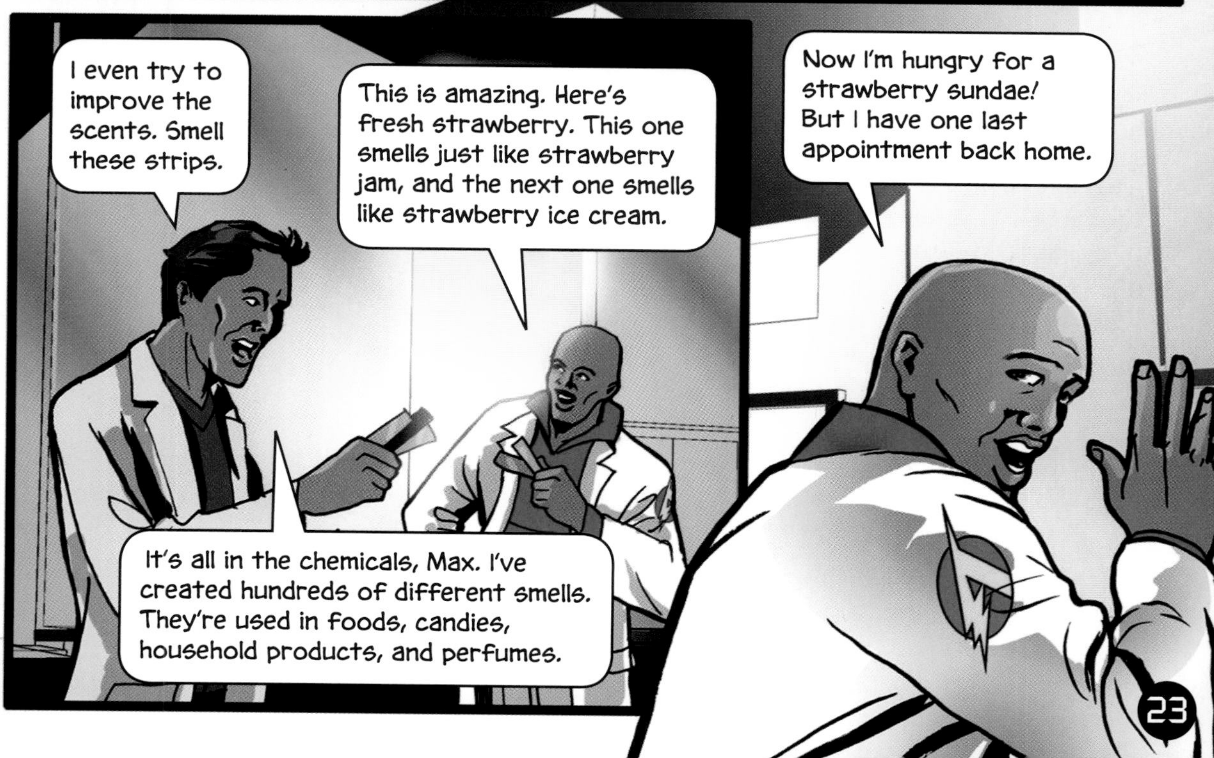
I even try to improve the scents. Smell these strips.
This is amazing. Here's fresh strawberry. This one smells just like strawberry jam, and the next one smells like strawberry ice cream.
It's all in the chemicals, Max. I've created hundreds of different smells. They're used in foods, candies, household products, and perfumes.
Now I'm hungry for a strawberry sundae! But I have one last appointment back home.

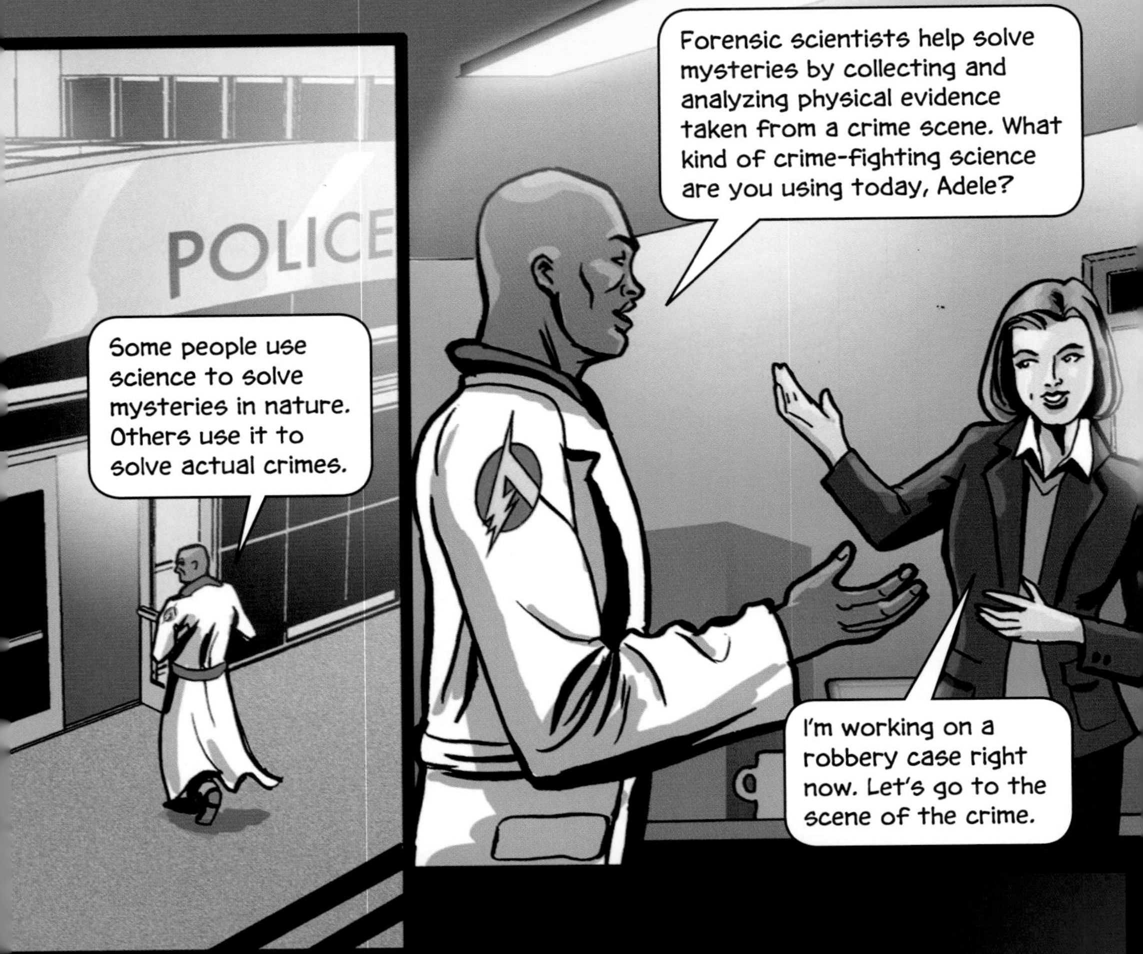

Some people use science to solve mysteries in nature. Others use it to solve actual crimes.
POLICE
Forensic scientists help solve mysteries by collecting and analyzing physical evidence taken from a crime scene. What kind of crime-fighting science are you using today, Adele?
I'm working on a robbery case right now. Let's go to the scene of the crime.

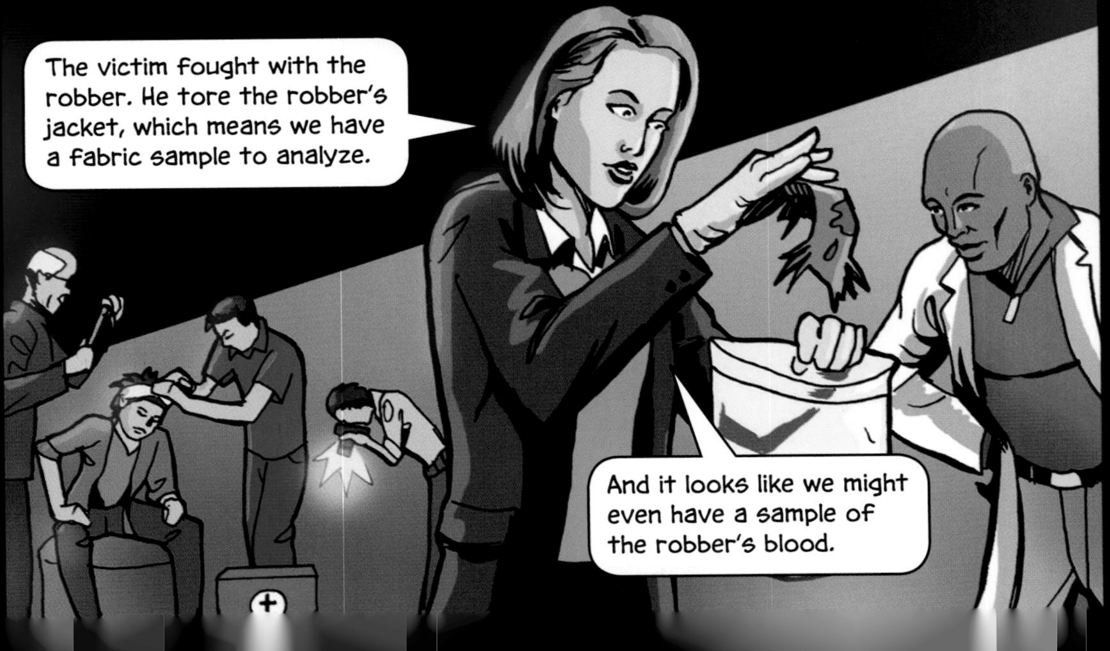

The victim fought with the robber. He tore the robber's jacket, which means we have a fabric sample to analyze.
And it looks like we might even have a sample of the robber's blood.

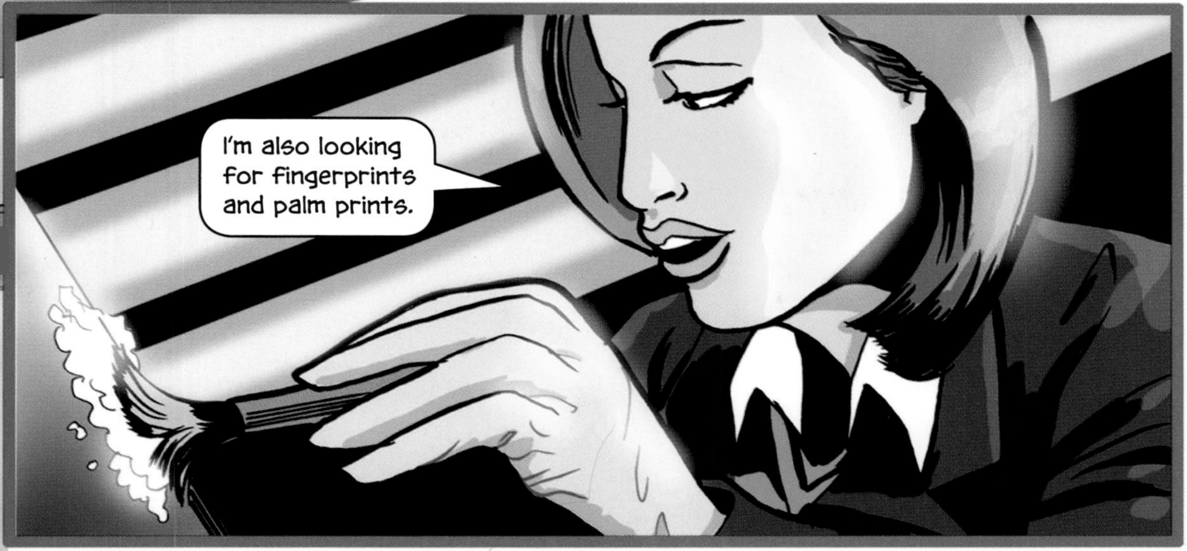
I'm also looking for fingerprints and palm prints.

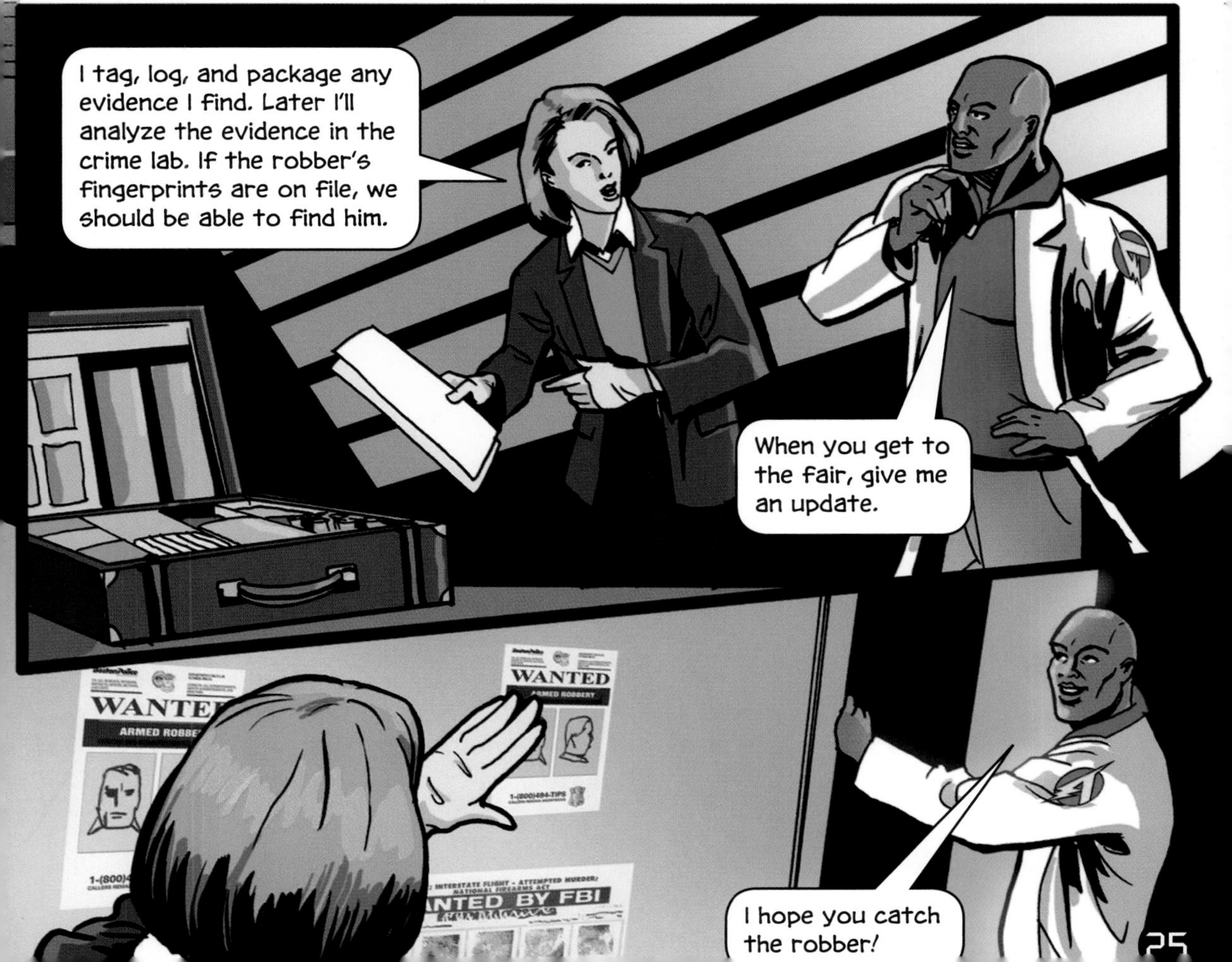
I tag, log, and package any evidence I find. Later I'll analyze the evidence in the crime lab. If the robber's fingerprints are on file, we should be able to find him.
When you get to the fair, give me an update.
WANTED
ARMED ROBBERY
1-(800)494-TIPS
I hope you catch the robber!

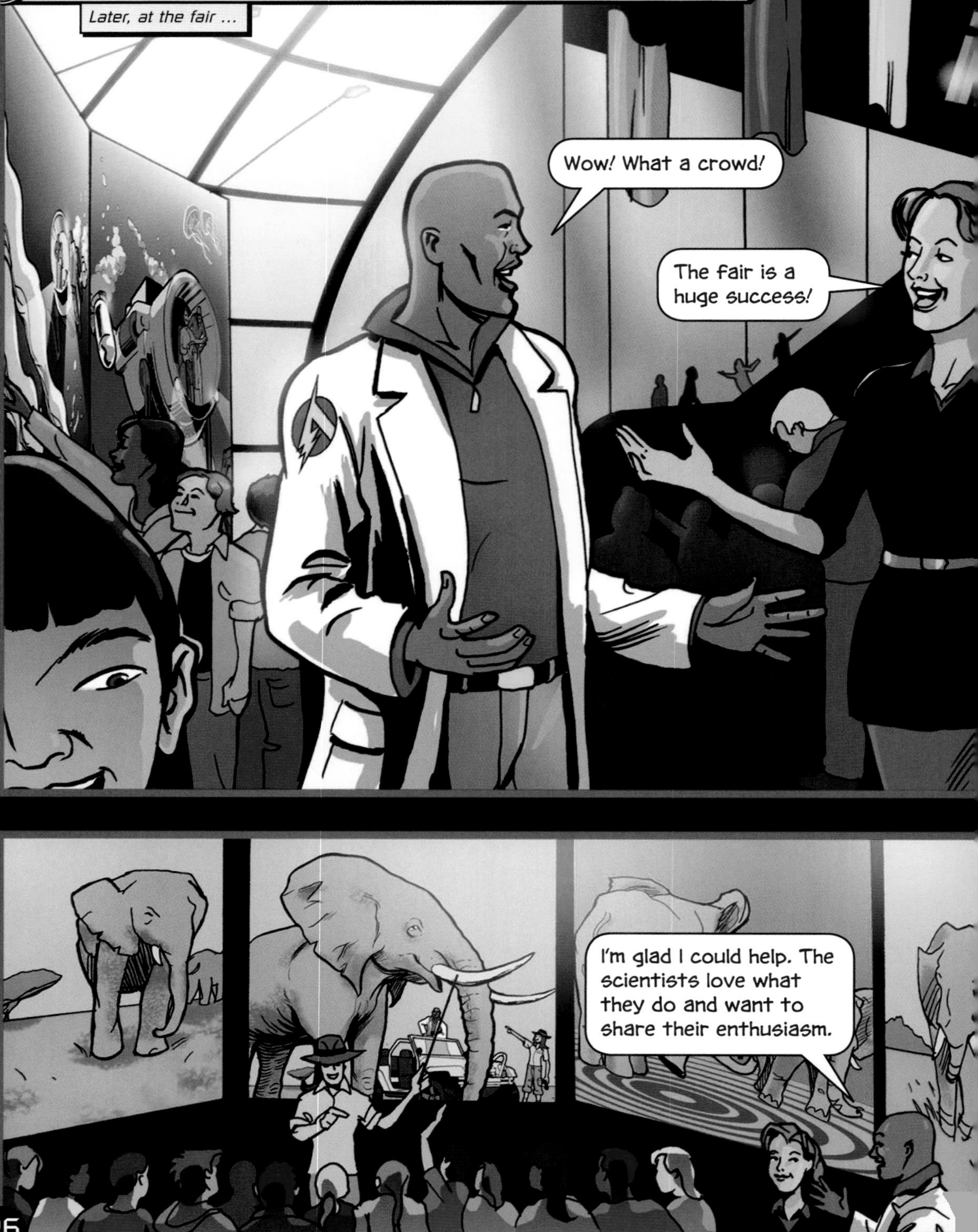
Later, at the fair ...
Wow! What a crowd!
The fair is a huge success!
I'm glad I could help. The scientists love what they do and want to share their enthusiasm.

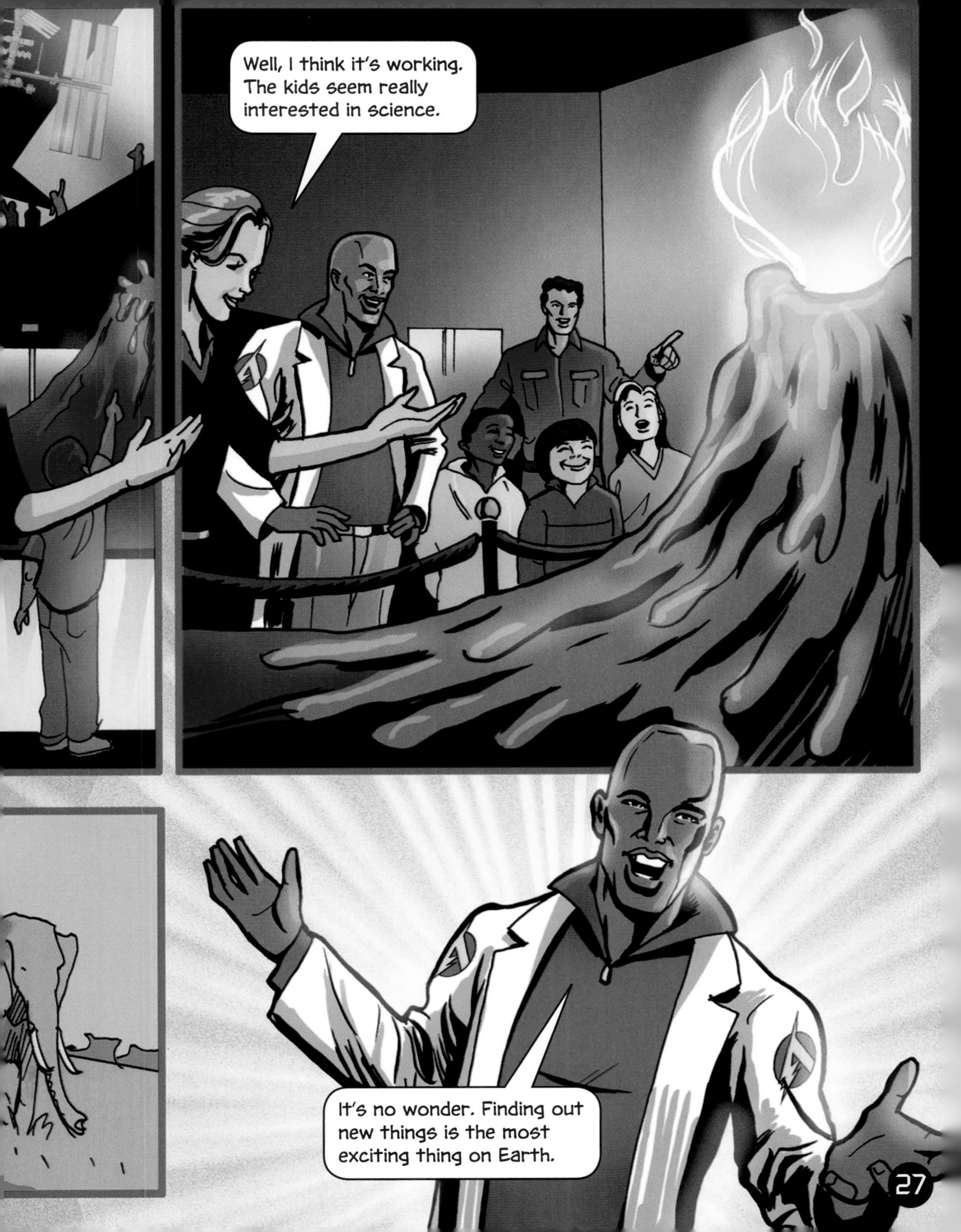
Well, I think it's working. The kids seem really interested in science.
It's no wonder. Finding out new things is the most exciting thing on Earth.

Climatologists drill down thousands of feet to remove cores of ice from ancient glaciers. They look for bubbles of air trapped inside. The air tells them the levels of different gases found in the ancient atmosphere. Scientists now know that today's air is choked with carbon dioxide gas, which causes global warming. The atmosphere has around 30 times more carbon dioxide than at any time in the past 800,000 years. By 2100, levels may be higher than in the past 10 million years.

Vaccines boost the immune system's natural ability to protect itself from disease-causing germs and even abnormal or diseased cells. Scientists have already created a few vaccines to help prevent and treat certain types of cancer. Researchers today are looking for safe and effective vaccines for a variety of diseases, including diabetes, HIV, and Alzheimer's.

Forensic scientists help solve crimes. Wildlife forensic scientists help solve crimes too—but in this case, the victim is an animal. Wildlife forensic cases often involve poachers. Scientists examine items such as blood and tissue samples, bones, teeth, fur, feathers, and stomach contents. Using what they find, they can determine what caused the animal's death.

Paleontologists study the remains of ancient plants and animals. Those remains, called fossils, tell us what life was like long ago.

Scientists called archaeologists try to learn about the past. These scientists study ancient civilizations. They search the globe to find out what people ate, what kinds of tools they used, and what their daily lives were like.

Astronomers study the universe outside Earth's atmosphere, including moons, comets, planets, stars, and galaxies. Some astronomers study how galaxies form. Others look for signs of life outside our planet or try to figure out how the universe itself came to be.

 Scientists called physicists study the tiniest particles known in the universe. All matter is made of atoms. Atoms can be broken down into even tinier particles, such as protons, neutrons, electrons, and quarks. Physicists smash these tiny particles together in huge machines called particle accelerators. This helps physicists learn more about why the universe looks and acts the way it does.

MORE ABOUT

SUPER SCIENTIST

Real name: Maxwell J. Axiom
Hometown: Seattle, Washington
Height: 6' 1"   Weight: 192 lbs
Eyes: Brown   Hair: None

Super capabilities: Super intelligence; able to shrink to the size of an atom; sunglasses give x-ray vision; lab coat allows for travel through time and space.

Origin: Since birth, Max Axiom seemed destined for greatness. His mother, a marine biologist, taught her son about the mysteries of the sea. His father, a nuclear physicist and volunteer park ranger, schooled Max on the wonders of earth and sky.

One day on a wilderness hike, a megacharged lightning bolt struck Max with blinding fury. When he awoke, Max discovered a newfound energy and set out to learn as much about science as possible. He traveled the globe earning degrees in every aspect of the field. Upon his return, he was ready to share his knowledge and new identity with the world. He had become Max Axiom, Super Scientist.

archaea (ar-KEY-uh)—a group of single-celled organisms; archaea are similar to bacteria and often live in extreme environments

bacteria (bak-TEER-ee-uh)—one-celled, microscopic living things that exist all around you and inside you; many bacteria are useful, but some cause disease

control group (kuhn-TROHL GROOP)—a group of test subjects not being treated; in an experiment, the control group is used to compare scientific results against a group that is treated

dropwindsonde (DROP-wind-sahnd)—a device that scientists drop into hurricanes and tropical storms to measure and study them

evidence (EV-uh-duhnss)—information, items, and facts that help prove something is true or false

gravity (GRAV-uh-tee)—a force that pulls objects with mass together; gravity pulls objects down toward the center of Earth

magma (MAG-muh)—melted rock found under the earth's surface

magnetic field (mag-NE-tik FEELD)—the space near a magnetic body or current-carrying body in which magnetic forces can be detected

orbit (OR-bit)—the path an object follows as it goes around the sun or a planet

seismometer (size-MAH-meter)—a machine used to measure earthquakes

solar storm (SOH-lurh STORM)—a burst of energy from the surface of the sun; solar storms can affect Earth's magnetic field

submersible (suhb-MURS-uh-buhl)—a small underwater craft powered by motors

vaccine (vak-SEEN)—a medicine that prevents a disease

READ MORE

Burns, Loree Griffin. *Citizen Scientists: Be a Part of Scientific Discovery from Your Own Backyard.* New York: H. Holt, 2012.

Davidson, Tish. *African American Scientists and Inventors.* Major Black Contributions from Emancipation to Civil Rights. Philadelphia: Mason Crest, 2013.

Hartman, Eve, and Wendy Meshbesher. *The Scientists Behind Medical Advances.* Sci-Hi Scientists. Chicago: Raintree, 2011.

Wheeler, Jill C. *Joanne Simpson: Magnificent Meteorologist.* Women in Science. Minneapolis: ABDO Pub., 2013.

INTERNET SITES

FactHound offers a safe, fun way to find Internet sites related to this book. All sites on FactHound have been researched by our staff.

Here's all you do:

Visit *www.facthound.com*

Type in this code: 9781429699365

archaea, 16
archaeologists, 28
astronomers, 9, 29
atmosphere, 28, 29

bacteria, 14, 15, 16, 17
blood samples, 21, 24, 28
botanists, 9

chemicals, 15, 20, 23
climatologists, 28

diseases, 15, 20
dropwindsonde, 10
drugs, 15

food chemists, 22–23
forensic scientists, 24–25, 28

International Space Station (ISS), 6, 7, 8

marine scientists, 16–17
meteorologist, 10–11
microbiologists, 14–15
microorganisms. *See* bacteria

paleontologists, 28
particle accelerators, 29
physicists, 29
physiologists, 8

samples, 12, 15, 21, 22, 24, 28
seismologists, 13
seismometers, 13
solar storms, 9

vaccines, 21, 28
virologists, 19, 20–21
volcanologist, 11, 12–13

wildlife forensic scientists, 28

zoologists, 18–19